Managing Mathematics

A Handbook for the Head of Department

Also published in cooperation with the Mathematical Association:

132 Short Programs for the Mathematical Classroom

Maths Talk

Sharing Mathematics with Parents

Managing Mathematics

A Handbook for the Head of Department

The Mathematical Association and
Stanley Thornes (Publishers) Ltd

First published 1988 by
Stanley Thornes (Publishers) Ltd,
Old Station Drive,
Leckhampton,
CHELTENHAM GL53 0DN

British Library Cataloguing in Publication Data.

Managing mathematics: a handbook for
heads of maths departments.
1. Schools. Curriculum subjects:
Mathematics. Teaching.
I. Mathematical Association
510′.7′1

ISBN 0-85950-918-4

Typeset by Tech-Set, Gateshead, Tyne & Wear
Printed and bound in Great Britain at The Bath Press, Avon

Dedication

To present and future generations of heads of mathematics departments who undertake an increasingly demanding job.

Contents

Chairman's Foreword x

Acknowledgements xii

1 *Prelude: On becoming a Head of Department – reflections on the role* 1

2 *Implementing the curriculum* 13

Planning the curriculum 14
The teaching approach 17
Written statements of curriculum policy 19
Monitoring implementation 20
Assessment 21
The evolving curriculum 22
Conclusions – in the real world 23

3 *Concern with pupils* 24

Chris Rigby's mathematical education – the needs 25
Teaching groups 28
Particular needs 32
Conclusion 40

4 *Concern with colleagues* 41

What type of leader? 42
Handling diversity in the departmental team 43
Appointing staff 50
Professional development 54
Career progression 56
Conclusion 61

5 *Administration* 62

Communication 62
Finance 66
The management of books and resources 68
Allocation of staff to teaching groups 70
Internal assessment 71
External examinations 73
Staff records 74
Pupil records 75
Bumph, filing and memory 75
Teaching rooms 76
General working conditions for staff 78

6 *Beyond the department* 80

The hierarchy within the educational system 80
Other departments 84
Other services within the school 86
Other schools 86
Parents 87
Employers 88
Training institutions 90
Examination boards 92
Teachers' centres 93
Professional associations 94
Conclusion 95

Postscript: 96

Meeting of the publications committee

Appendices

(The first digit corresponds to the numbering of the chapters in the book.)

1 *Reflections of experience as a head of department* 98

2 *Implementing the curriculum*

2.1 Purpose, aims and objectives in teaching mathematics 101
2.2 Some ideas for implementing goal 42 (*Why, What and How?* MA, 1976) 106
2.3 Assessment schemes in mathematics 108
2.4 A summary of GCSE coursework structures in the five examining groups 114

3 *Concern with pupils*

3.1 Advice to Heads of Department from *Girls and Mathematics* - Royal Society/IMA 116

4 *Concern with colleagues*

4.1 Personal characteristics of managers in schools 118
4.2 Student teachers at Hartcliffe School 119
4.3 Job specifications for mathematical posts 121

5 *Administration*

5.1 Section headings of a typical departmental handbook 124
5.2 Considering a new textbook 125
5.3 Departmental responsibilities 126
5.4 Internal examinations 127

6 *Beyond the department*

6.1 Preliminary checklist of mathematics inquiries from the Science Department 128
6.2 Council for the Accreditation of Teacher Education 129

7 *Sources and resources*

Books 133
Journals 136
Materials for mathematics teaching 138
Posters 139
Audio visual material 139
Organisations involved in mathematics education 140

8 *An invitation to join the Mathematical Association* 143

Glossary 146

Chairman's Foreword

When *Mathematics Counts* finally came off the presses in 1982, the Mathematical Association was ready, willing and waiting to respond. As so many members of the committee of inquiry were active members of the Mathematical Association, little time had to be spent on preliminary discussions before work could begin.

'Waiting for Cockcroft' had become the chief occupation of many involved in mathematics education and it was with great relief that work on many projects could now begin in earnest, supported by mention in one of the report's hallowed paragraphs.

The crucial importance of developing the role of the Head of Department was emphasised in several chapters. The Mathematical Association felt that it should play its part in developing the materials and courses needed to help Heads of Department and those aspiring to this position to develop the skills that are required.

Three initiatives were launched by the Mathematical Association at that time and others have started since:

> The Diploma Board spawned a new group which developed a Head of Department Diploma.
>
> The Mini-Conference Committee held popular and successful conferences for Heads of Department chiefly attended by those who sought promotion to Head of Department.
>
> The Teaching Committee set up the Handbook sub-committee which has produced this book.

The Handbook project, as many before it, has been rather longer in gestation than in conception. We soon discovered that running a department was one thing, writing about it quite another. The final pages are being written as GCSE candidates prepare for the first examinations (only ten years after the Waddell Committee proposed their introduction to Parliament). Inevitably our Handbook will be less than specific on some contentious and still unfolding current issues (e.g. the national mathematics curriculum, forms of pupil assessment, teacher appraisal, contracts of employment and directed time) but we do not apologise for concentrating on those fundamental management and human skills required of a Head of Department which are ever present elements of the task. We have concentrated on providing plenty of helpful advice from practising Heads of Department, leavened by the influence of advisers, lecturers and other teachers.

As chairman of the group, I am indebted to the four members of the group who joined me in the task of getting everything written down and especially to John Hayter who as editor has succeeded in giving both uniformity and clarity to our disparate efforts. We are grateful to all those who gave advice and criticism. Without their help it would have been finished in half the time, but would not have had one quarter its value!

For errors, omissions and any pieces of downright bad advice we, of course, accept full responsibility.

Roy Ashley
January 1988

The text was written by:

Roy Ashley (Chairman)	Head of Mathematics, Wootton Upper School, Bedfordshire.
Jim Edwards	Head of Mathematics. Branston School, Lincolnshire.
John Hayter (Editor)	Senior Lecturer, School of Education, Bristol University.
Bob Shaw	County Adviser for Mathematics, Hertfordshire.
Gerald South	Head of Mathematics, Trinity School, Croydon.

Acknowledgements

Those who undertook the writing of the handbook wish to thank and to acknowledge the vital contribution made by many people in the preparation of this book. In particular:

Catherine Sarson and other members who attended early discussions of the project

Teachers, advisers and lecturers who contributed their own ideas or materials used in their schools

Members of the Association who commented on draft chapters

Institutions who allowed the writing committee to use their premises for meetings: Polytechnic of Central London, William Tyndale Teachers' Centre, University of Bristol, London University Institute of Education

The following schools who agreed to have photographs taken: Backwell, Chew Valley, Churchill, The Grange, Nailsea, Newent

Mike George, for taking the photographs

Carole Baker and colleagues in the School of Education, Bristol University for their cheerful, patient and reliable help in typing and other production matters

Clevedon School, for allowing some of the photographs to be taken, including the cover.

The Institute of Mathematics and its Applications with The Royal Society, for permission to use an extract from *Girls and Mathematics* (1986)

1 Prelude: On becoming a head of department – reflections on the role

Early March

> Dear Mr Smith,
>
> The Exshire Education Authority is pleased to offer you the post of Head of Mathematics at Bucklands Comprehensive School with effect 1 September 1988. The salary will be . . .

So this is it. After eight applications, three interviews including two full days of grilling at Bucklands, the offer of the job I have been aiming at for twelve years since starting my teaching career. Having made the decision to teach in the final years of my mathematics degree course, I knew this was what I wanted to become – in contact with my subject *and* in charge. Perhaps I shall go higher in the system, but the job of a deputy head has never seemed particularly attractive to me. Anyway, further thoughts in that direction can wait.

Another six months before starting – time to think, to read, to find out how to do all those things said easily (but with conviction!) at interview. Time to pick a few brains, to visit some other schools, maybe attend the Mathematical Association Conference! Would it be a good idea to apply for a day or two's leave to spend at the new school before the year ends? The adviser seemed approachable – at least after the interview – perhaps it would be worth talking to her.

During the early hours next morning after the celebration

What have I let myself in for? The head seemed pretty detached and the internal applicant who was disappointed could be a major problem. Mathematics at the school didn't look to be exactly thriving and the department seemed to be in a deep rut. The rooms in which the subject is taught are scattered and I can't recall seeing anything in the rooms to inspire or encourage mathematical thinking. Mr McBain seems to have defected from the department to teach Computer Studies and has taken the computers with him. Why did the deputy headmistress ask how I would relate my innovative ideas to mature teachers with well established practice? Did they say falling rolls would mean the redeployment of seven staff next year? The textbooks were in a tatty state, I wonder if we could introduce . . .

Light dawns

What kind of preparation have I had for this new job? Working in two very different departments has helped, I guess. Terry Squires was a great support in my first years. He gave me a lot of time but we all worked independently in his department. One meeting a term and an annual party was about the extent of our departmental life. Ambition having driven me to accept a Scale 3 post at Amberfield, I have experienced an alternative style of leadership. Jeremy Tripp is clearly on the way to the top – if he has any say in the matter. Meetings are held, paper flows, orders are given and parents are left in no doubt that Mr Tripp runs a tight ship with their children's mathematical education in good hands. The exam results are incredible and the staff feel secure – providing they agree with Jeremy. Needless to say we avoid having student teachers messing up the works. There's precious little contact with anyone outside the school in fact. Jeremy has mainly scathing comment for those in the advisory service and as for training institutions – a haven for incompetents he said on receiving an unsolicited account of some local development activity. I have attended one or two courses which have stimulated my thinking. A post-Cockcroft series at the university started me exploring more open mathematical activities. The response of the pupils has really surprised me – some most unlikely characters have become really involved and we generated some good display work. GCSE should give such an approach some impetus – until recently to talk about such approaches in our department was likely to be regarded as subversive activity. I sense Jeremy is concerned, particularly now that our lively probationer is sharing my enthusiasm. A good time to leave I guess.

But twelve years in schools doesn't seem to have given me much preparation for managing a team of twelve mathematics teachers (+ a few bits), for becoming responsible for the mathematical education of 1500 pupils, for participating in the inter-departmental discussions on curriculum and other issues. Hasn't it occurred to anyone that this is a crazy way to run a show? From my experience to date it doesn't seem all that clear what is expected of a head of department. Somebody ought to write a guide! Someone has mentioned special courses for HoDs but if there aren't any courses in this part of the country, I could at least find out what those with whom I shall be working think. Might be worth a letter to a few people asking for their views, for example a headmaster, an adviser, a college tutor, an experienced head of department, perhaps even an ordinary teacher!

> Dear
>
> I have recently been appointed Head of Mathematics at Bucklands Comprehensive School in Exshire. I wonder if you could assist me by sending me a few remarks on how you see the job of a head of department . . .

While waiting

Cockcroft must have said something? Quite a bit according to the index!

The Head of Department

507 We believe that the Head of Department has a crucial role to play in implementing the matters to which we have already drawn attention. Unless he or she provides positive and sustained leadership and direction for the mathematics department it will not operate as effectively as it might do and the pupils will be correspondingly disadvantaged.

508 In our view, the Head of Department should be responsible for

- the production and up-dating of suitable schemes of work;
- the organisation of the department and of its teaching resources;
- the monitoring of the teaching within the department and of the work and assessment of pupils;
- playing a full part in the professional development and in-service training of those who teach mathematics;
- liaison with other departments in the school and with other schools and colleges in the area.

In setting out this list we are aware that it does not, of itself, relate specifically to mathematics and we regard the responsibilities we have identified as being among those which should be undertaken by heads of all subject departments. However, we consider that, among heads of department, the Head of Mathematics has a task which can be especially difficult and demanding.

Over the next few weeks

The Headmaster writes:

I am a mathematician, so my expectation of a head of department bears that stamp. When I was a head of department I was also under a mathematician headmaster: he gave me absolute freedom, did not interfere or comment except when invited; he was stimulating and very up to date. I try to emulate his example, which I still admire, but I am aware that I could be regarded as a brooding presence - I hope I am not.

So much for my wish for my senior mathematician's view of me. What do I expect of her?

First and foremost I expect her to stand up to me intellectually, to be willing to argue a mathematical and pedagogical case with me and to make decisions on sound intellectual lines disregarding my advice and opinion if need be. The important element is intellectual rigour which all can appreciate and admire, find congenial and stimulating, persuasive and demanding of loyalty.

Second I expect her personal relations with pupils, mathematical colleagues, other colleagues, parents *et al*. to be first class: her style to be without question *primus inter pares* laced with plenty of discussion.

Third, I expect her managerial skills over curricula, accommodation, equipment, books and materials, pupils and mathematical colleagues to be second nature - there, unobtrusive, but effective.

Finally, I expect her to hold her ground with mathematical professors, HMI, examiners, *et al*. and to carry the arguments into their courts using her own mathematical skills and administrative and teaching experience to provide the foundation of self confidence.

THINKS

Intellectual rigour sounds daunting and hardly the outcome of my sessions with our low attainers group in the fourth year. Perhaps it's as well I'm not going there!

The local adviser replies using the word processor facilities of his micro-computer:

'What makes a good maths department?' Responses to the standard interview question will differ but there will be little doubt in the interviewers' mind that the most important factor is the quality of the Head of Department. That person will shape the professional outlook of the department in much the same way as a head teacher establishes the individuality of a school. The recruitment of Head of Department must thus be regarded as a matter of the utmost importance and the local authority will normally wish to be involved in the selection procedures. Such procedures will probe a candidate's educational outlook, awareness of current developments in mathematics education and, not least, the intended style of leadership. Of prime importance is the Head teacher's judgement regarding the extent to which the personalities of particular candidates will complement those of existing senior members of staff.

The interviewing panel will be aware that a head of department can, in the words of HMI 'frequently underestimate the need for positive leadership'. On the other hand there is also the possibility of an over-zealous style of leadership which can verge towards the autocratic. The panel will therefore try to form a picture of an applicant's style of leadership and to judge whether there are qualities of personality which would enable the successful candidate to work successfully with both departmental colleagues and with more senior staff.

A local authority necessarily carries overall responsibility for the quality of curricular provision in its schools. Within a particular school, that responsibility rests with the Head teacher who will delegate appropriately to head of departments. Thus the Head will look to such staff not only to take a lead in establishing professional policy and practice within their respective departments but to monitor the success with which that policy is implemented. It will be expected that they will have sufficient involvement in and awareness of the full breadth of work of their department to ensure that they are the first to perceive impending difficulty and to take early action. In serious cases, a head of department should not delay alerting the Head of the situation. Some difficulties, such as those involving serious professional shortcomings of a teacher, may call for the mathematics adviser or another officer of the local authority to be involved.

Such an approach to representatives of the local authority will usually be made by the Head teacher following consultations with and advice from the Head of Department. The successful discharge of such responsibilities by the Head of Department clearly calls for a detailed knowledge not only of the programme of work within the department but of the success with which individual members of the department are responding to that programme.

The Head of Department will be expected to affirm strongly the claim of mathematics for a reasonable share of the material and human resources available within the school. At the same time, it will be expected that a head of department will also have a perception of the needs of the schools as a whole and thus be able to judge the needs of mathematics in proper relation to those of other areas of the curriculum.

THINKS

Seeing maths in relation to the demands of other subjects will be a novel experience. Not since college days have I had to 'justify the place of mathematics in the whole school curriculum'.

The college tutor's reply was next to arrive:

The aspects of the Head of Department's role which relate most closely to the colleges are: dealing with students in initial training who are placed in the department for teaching practice, care of the probationer and involvement in staff development or in-service education. I will comment briefly on each of these aspects.

Most schools have a member of staff, usually Head or Deputy, who has overall responsibility for the arrangement of teaching practice in that school. However, in secondary schools it is invariably the Head of Department in the student's main subject who has the greatest influence over the success or failure of the practice. He (or she) needs to be sensitive to the delicate balance between support for a person who is, after all, *practising* a difficult and complicated job, and the fact that the student will develop only if given the opportunity to make his own decisions and face the consequences. While the Head of Department's major concern is for the children who are learning mathematics in his department, he must offer the student the chance to make experiments and to take reasonable risks. In mathematics especially, there may be differences between the teaching methods which are standard in the department and those which the college has advocated, and some compromise must be negotiated. A programme has to be devised to include teaching of classes which offer a range of experience, as well as a variety of opportunity for observation. And finally, the Head of Department has to arrange a suitable system of monitoring the student's progress over the practice as a whole, with the consequent switch between the contrasting roles of counsellor and assessor.

When students begin to seek teaching posts, colleges are concerned to try to place them in schools where their probationary period is as productive as possible. Many successful teachers of mathematics can testify to the wide gulf between teaching practice and the first year as a full-time, paid teacher and the very great difficulties which they experienced during that year. The sheer weight of preparation, marking, establishing relationships with many new colleagues and children is a daunting task which needs considerable support from established staff and especially the relevant Head of Department. There is a sense in which students gain shelter under the temporary nature of a teaching practice, which is denied them by the permanence and extra responsibilities of a teaching post, and it is largely due to the Head of Department to guide them through this induction period. Specifically, they need clear explanations of the department's organisation and their part in it; guidance in appropriate syllabuses and teaching methods for each class and the resources available to them; and the standards expected within the department. They need advice on the assessment of pupils' work and record keeping, particularly where these records are communicated to other teachers. Without this important extension to initial education, a probationer's chances of becoming an effective teacher are considerably reduced.

Staff development of the department's members is becoming increasingly a matter of significance with relative immobility and lack of opportunities for promotion leading to frustration and consequent lowering of morale. Those departments which attend to staff development find that it can counter such feelings by offering wider horizons for the work available to each member. The most fruitful work seems to be that done in school by the department as a whole, often, but by no means always, with a college lecturer or LEA adviser acting as a catalyst and an outside commentator. Other methods are by attendance at DES, LEA or college in-service courses, ranging from one year full-time secondment to five weekly sessions of two hours or a one-day conference. The Head of Department can be a great facilitator for such development by making his staff aware of all possibilities as the publicity comes into the school, and following up with firmer suggestions where he sees particular advantage in matching a member of staff with a particular course. Most colleges are able and willing to respond to initiatives from their local schools related to staff development needs, and can often be a most useful resource for such activities.

In each of these aspects the Head of Department has a unique role to play, and in the college view, time given from his meagre stock of non-teaching time is time well spent.

THINKS

I like the 'meagre stock of non-teaching time' bit. All this sounds a tall order in three additional free periods! The attitude to student teachers sounds realistic and sympathetic – I can't remember my tutor being like that.

Several teachers gave their views and in many cases vented their feelings about the shortcomings of their present head of department. In summary the following points were made:

1. *To help and support members of the department in relation to:*
   a) *Pupils*; both with their content and method of teaching, and with discipline
   b) *Staff outside the department*; those with particular responsibilities, also probationers and students
   c) *Staff within the department*; those with particular responsibilities, also probationers and students

d) *People outside the school*; for example parents, governors, advisers

2. *To serve as a model*
   a) Being a competent mathematician and an effective teacher
   b) Being willing to allow his/her lessons to be observed
   c) Having his own work and classes well organised
   d) Being prepared to admit that he has made a mistake or doesn't know the answer or lacks a particular skill
   e) Being seen to be fair in dealing with the department e.g. in the distribution of the classes on the timetable
   f) Being sympathetic yet firm in dealing with pupils and colleagues and prepared to take difficult/unpopular decisions

3. *Administrative duties*
   a) To hold frequent and regular meetings of the department
   b) To ensure purposeful yet open meetings which give members a sense of achievement from their contributions being valued and a sense of progress
   c) To delegate responsibilities
   d) To organise departmental resources efficiently

4. *Accessibility/Interest*
   a) To be prepared to give time to listen and to help an individual
   b) To be open to suggestions both from individuals and within departmental discussions
   c) To be supportive of individual initiative

5. *Professional development*
   To be aware of career structures and possibilities for professional development for staff

6. *To exhibit superhuman qualities*

THINKS

The last expectation gives me hope.
They will soon know that I'm not superhuman but I *have* come to stay!

Last to arrive after some six weeks, a reply from the Head of Department:

Thanks for your enquiry about how I see my role. Can't say I've had much time to think about it, though your letter did prompt me to speculate on whether I have the balance between "thinking and initiating' as opposed to "responding' anywhere near right. To show you what I mean I kept a diary yesterday.

1. Phone call at home, 7.30 a.m.; colleague ill; I hope the exercises he has suggested for his sets are suitable; at least it will give me a chance to look in on his 3rd form to see how they are getting on.

2. Arrive school; 2nd former wants to know (or his Dad does) what computer he should buy; I wish I had time to keep up with all the latest models; but is it really my responsibility? Computing does not equal maths after all.

3. Register my group; no absence note from Barnes; Davies wants a reference for a Saturday job; I have not yet found out who broke the chair in here yesterday; should HoDs have to be tutors?

4. HM informs of new pupil - which set? I will ask Barry to assess him, I trust his judgement; how nice it is to delegate.

5. Pupil has lost textbook; how much will it cost, where did I put that catalogue which arrived the other day, I must get a box file for them; why are there no spare copies in the book room? I wonder if . . . is sitting on a pile of them in his room again?

6. HM wants to discuss external examination results (I knew this would come) - bang goes another free period.

7. At the end of discussion HM shows me letter from parent complaining about the maths teaching (or lack of it) his son is getting; that's going to mean another prickly session with . . . , he is so defensive about these queries. I wonder why?

8. I must now work through that problem my probationary teacher could not do; it looks easy enough, perhaps there is a catch; I suppose we all have our blind spots.

9. Lunch time; 6th former wants to know which university is best for maths - what does 'best' mean? My knowledge is very second-hand; what can I do to answer this question more sensibly in the future? A quick bite to eat then it will be time for Junior Maths Club; I feel I

am running out of ideas here, why don't I involve one or two other members of the department? Over lunch a casual comment from a colleague suggests that perhaps the 2nd form syllabus has not been made as clear as perhaps it should - but why do some assume that because it's in the textbook it must be taught (and vice versa)?

10. 4 p.m. end of afternoon school - yet another board's syllabus proposals in my pigeon hole. Head of Chemistry approaches, pupils can't do simple proportion; what does he mean by 'simple'; at least hockey practice gives me an excuse for running away. When I've marked the 4th year books this evening I must start thinking about next year's timetable.

This might be a better description of a HoD's life than any management-minded head will give you! On the whole, though, I enjoy it. The sense of driving one's own bus, the contacts outside the department and the continual unexpectedness of humanity make it stimulating and on the whole satisfying. Welcome to the club and all good wishes.

THINKS

Phew, I'd better get my role clear before being sucked into the whirlwind.

Late summer term

Exam classes departed, a little space to review the perceptions of different groups and establish a sense of direction. I guess another group of representative individuals in the profession would have given different answers. Nevertheless there has been plenty to set me thinking.

I still feel intellectually underprepared for the job. The curriculum and management issues need study in some depth but there hasn't been time or opportunity. I shall have to survive on the intellectual alacrity and what information I can glean from reading and contacts. The latter seem important, senior staff, professional colleagues in the school and outside who can act as a sounding board, source of information, salvation, etc.

The expectations of the members of the department are daunting. Did I ever expect so much? It certainly wasn't/isn't there in departments where I've worked. Establishing the right kind of relationship is going to be vital from the start. They will feel uncertain about a new 'boss'. Can I both reassure them, yet start the show moving in 'my' direction from the start? If I can get the balance of confidence and competence right initially, we shall be in with a chance.

My leadership style must derive in part from the person I am, as well as the nature of the job. It might be worth talking this aspect out further with Jenny Bracewell our professional tutor; she will be prepared to act as a mirror and adviser.

There's no way I can cope with all the tasks which any group seem to find easy to construct. It will have to be a team effort. I guess we shall become a team most quickly if we recognise a common purpose. With a bit of luck they may be concerned about some of the aspects of the department's work which already worry me – ear to the ground! That, together with a demonstrated openness in what I do and a concern for a responsiveness to what they think, may offer the best bonding agent. Whatever happens I'm sure that I shall be asking for more effort from them (and myself). Their willingness to give more will undoubtedly stem from their feelings about it being worthwhile in their terms. Their terms may be in relation to their professional views and experience and their other pressing commitments. The former can certainly grow if given the opportunity. The relationship between what is right for the individual teacher within a department and what is good for pupils is complex. But perhaps unscrambling that is a lifetime's work of a HoD. So, maybe a short list of guidelines is all that I should distil at this stage from the advice and the thinking.

I want:

i) To establish a departmental team which is mutually supportive, intellectually stimulating and actively engaged in developing its professional competence in involving young people with mathematics.

ii) To use my experience, knowledge and position of authority within the department to provide support, to give encouragement, to demonstrate a valuing of each person's contribution and when necessary to challenge and take action if issues of professional neglect or malpractice arise.

iii) To build a strong departmental framework by establishing:
- a sense of purpose through a developing philosophy, shared experience, awareness of problems and willingness to explore both ideas and practice
- a clearly documented but still developing curriculum philosophy and plan for the guidance of team members
- a lively departmental office which encourages a sense of identity and provides opportunity for informal passing of ideas
- a regular departmental forum not dominated by administrative matters
- a well identified set of mathematics teaching rooms
- a well organised resource base.

iv) To represent the department in a positive way both in the school and outside in the best interests of both the department and the school.

v) To continue to enjoy teaching across the ability and age range.

vi) To have some life out of school – for the sake of my family and my sanity.

I wonder how this list will look in twelve months time. Pretty naive I expect. Never mind there's a house move to organise, a holiday to take and then on 1 September, Bucklands here I come.

'Leaving?' – Appendix 1 contains an article (originally published in *Mathematics Teaching* No. 120) by Peter Stockwell reflecting on six years as Head of Mathematics at Montsaye School in Northamptonshire.

2 Implementing the curriculum

The mathematics curriculum is not a static entity. The plethora of discussion documents and reports from various agencies which have descended on schools during the past decade provide strong evidence for this categorical statement. However at any stage in the evolution of the mathematics curriculum, we are faced by the major challenges (a) of defining the curriculum with sufficient clarity and (b) of implementing it effectively within our schools. In this chapter we shall concentrate mainly on the factors and strategies that can help to encourage colleagues towards an appropriate, implemented curriculum.

If terminology is to help rather than hinder, it will be worthwhile from the outset to distinguish between the terms 'curriculum' and 'syllabus'. The Cockcroft Report (para. 438) uses the term 'syllabus' to denote a list of mathematical topics to be studied and the term 'curriculum' to include the whole mathematical experience of the pupil – in other words, both what is taught and how it is taught. We shall use the terms in this way in the discussion which follows.

Concern for the quality of curricular provision in this dual sense of content and teaching approach has to be regarded as fundamental in considering our multiple responsibilities. Tradition within a particular school may exert a strong influence on the nature of the existing curriculum. The content may be specified in a tangible form by a printed departmental syllabus. The methodology is perhaps less explicitly defined, but may be even more rigidly practised by colleagues who, through long experience and shortage of time and opportunity to explore alternatives, have developed personal and often restricted styles and strategies. To this situation, new heads of department will bring ideas of their own arising from their own philosophy and from experience in other schools.

In addition to these internal influences on the curriculum, it is apparent that agencies external to the school are exerting increasing influence on the mathematics curriculum. In the maintained sector, local authorities have their own curriculum statements for mathematics. For GCSE there are National Criteria which set out the essential requirements for all syllabuses for mathematics within the new examination framework. The Cockcroft Report established some fundamental principles concerning the teaching of mathematics at all levels. Her Majesty's Inspectors in their document *Mathematics from 5 to 16* set out a framework within which each school might develop a mathematics programme appropriate to its own pupils. The proposed mathematics curriculum within the framework of a National

Curriculum is the latest and most prescriptive in a long series of curriculum recommendations. Thus when a mathematics department in a secondary school sets out to design a mathematics curriculum for its pupils, it has to take account of the contents of such documents as well as reconciling the needs and traditions in the school and the current views within the department. A formidable challenge indeed!

It is very rare for a HoD to be planning a curriculum from scratch as might be the case in a new school. For most, the exercise is in the form of a review carried out while the present system is being serviced and maintained. Further, with the exception of fortunate HoDs seconded for the purpose, most will not be in a position to redesign the whole system within a short time span. Our thinking about planning needs therefore to take account of this.

Planning the curriculum

The planning has to result in an implemented curriculum and not just a well-presented text which may serve only to impress governors and short stay visitors. Throughout planning therefore, an eye has to be kept on putting it into practice with the implications this has for (a) the form of the outcome and (b) the involvement of staff in the planning activity. As HoDs we have the challenge to provide the structure and sense of purpose for enquiry, discussion and decision making, while enabling genuine participation by colleagues. Clearly stated aims provide an essential basis for the construction of a curriculum.

Preparing a list of aims is no easy task if they are to provide useful guidance in detailed planning and if they are to be a framework for evaluating the success of implementation. For example the aim 'Pupils shall extend their mathematical skills beyond those achieved at primary school' may be true in one sense, but seems of limited value in practice. On the other hand 'To provide continuity in a pupil's mathematical development from primary school through the secondary school' is an aim which, although general, is also challenging (a) to being informed about practice in mathematics in feeder schools and (b) to ways of recognising and meeting major differences in attainment throughout the secondary stage.

At some stage it will be necessary to be more specific in specifying what the teaching programme is intended to achieve. However, highly specific behavioural objectives can be inhibiting when planning and may well incorporate a view of pupil learning in small sequential steps which is highly dubious and not consistent with much currently recommended practice. In its earlier publication *Why, What and How?*, the Mathematical Association used the term 'goals' for more specific aims. 'Objectives' which are of a more general kind than highly specific behavioural objectives are still found of value in specifying intentions in particular parts of the curriculum. Appendix 2.1 provides some examples of statements of aims, goals and objectives which may act as a stimulus to thought on both content and form.

Even though a National Curriculum document for mathematics is likely to dominate thinking in the late eighties, the following will still provide important reference material when formulating aims and objectives:

Mathematics Counts (i.e. the Cockcroft Report)
Mathematics from 5 to 16 (HMI Discussion Document)
The National Criteria for GCSE
Why, What and How? (Mathematical Association)

Many relevant articles both practical and more theoretical have appeared in mathematics teaching journals. These can be most easily traced using the booklets *References of Use to Teachers of Mathematics*, published by the Centre for Studies in Science and Mathematics Education, University of Leeds.

Agreeing a set of aims may be a major achievement – indeed if there is too ready agreement in the department, it probably indicates that either the aims are too vague or that colleagues are not very involved! Once established, such aims can help resolve difficult problems, for example assisting the identification of redundant content in the syllabus and providing criteria for the inclusion of new material or activities. To help the overall aims permeate the sequential and more detailed planning, it can be useful to explore the ways in which one of the aims might be achieved. Appendix 2.2 is an example of the teacher's network of ideas with respect to the aim. 'The pupil should know about the contribution of some leading mathematicians and the historical development of some mathematical concepts.'

An aim does not offer a neat programme of teaching but it does open up possible activities which can be absorbed into a more timetabled approach. Asking members of the department to produce such a 'map' for an aim could make for a stimulating start to a departmental meeting or in-service day.

Another approach to setting the scene might be to ask members of the department to write on one side of an A4 sheet of paper an account of what they would like the five years of learning mathematics to be like at the school. Sharing such accounts would probably promote a lively and useful discussion. Putting them alongside the accounts written by fifth year pupils of various abilities would almost certainly add a whole new dimension to the debate!

Moving from agreed aims or listings such as those in *Mathematics from 5 to 16* to programmes for particular groups of pupils presents the real challenge.

During the seventies many departments produced their own workcards and other material – particularly for the lower school. The experience of such development activity was initially exciting but often the problems of production, quality and sheer pressure led many to look again at published materials. However, if a particular series of textbooks is used, the content and style of the texts may simply smother the attempts to achieve the identified aims. Figure 2.1 characterises two possible situations and strategies.

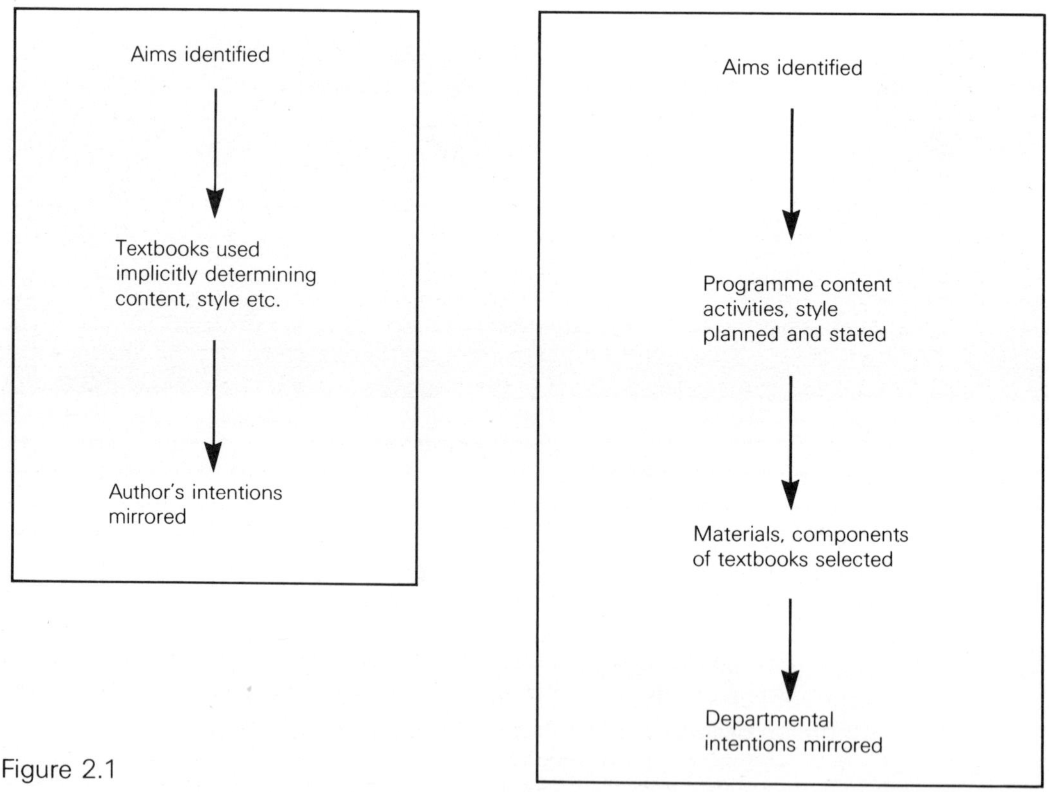

Figure 2.1

For most departments the production and use of such teaching programmes has the potential to be a real piece of school-based research and development.

To work on one or two particular areas in a first year of trials is probably desirable e.g. lower school maths (years 1 and 2), low attaining groups in years 4 and 5, first year A-level etc. This task is discussed in greater detail in 'Written statements of curriculum policy'.

The teaching approach

It is important that a department's consideration of the curriculum not only defines the content but also gives adequate attention to the teaching approach which is needed in order to fulfil the aims and objectives. The much quoted paragraph 243 of the Cockcroft Report proposes that successful teaching of mathematics should include six essential elements. It is interesting to note that these six have been immersed in a listing of twelve principles which HMI propose should govern classroom teaching approaches (see *Mathematics from 5 to 16* pp 35–44). The HMI list is as follows:

1. Needs perceived by the pupils
2. A firm conceptual basis
3. Flexibility
4. Encouragement to all pupils of both sexes and of all cultural backgrounds
5. Exposition by the teacher
6. Discussion
7. Appropriate practical work
8. Consolidation and practice of fundamental skills
9. Problem solving
10. Investigative work
11. Resources
12. Organisational arrangements

The task of guiding the teaching approaches of the whole department towards the intended curriculum offers the greatest challenge to our leadership skills. It is hoped that the following suggestions may be found to be helpful in this task.

i) If some colleagues are not currently working with the intended breadth of approach then it is fundamental that we should try to help them to do so on the basis of conviction rather than by coercion or through a sense of guilt.
ii) Observing other skilful teachers at work can be extremely helpful. A degree of co-operative teaching in the department can yield rich dividends. It may be best to start in a small way; a personal initiative in opening our classroom to others can usefully establish the principle of collaborative work in the classroom.
iii) Departmental meetings should regularly be concerned with the teaching approach. Asking a colleague to talk about an actual lesson given often has an immediacy which can be stimulating and effective. A short extract of a video made in a classroom can again provide a sense of reality with perhaps greater freedom to discuss the work of the unknown teacher. Key passages from national

PUMA

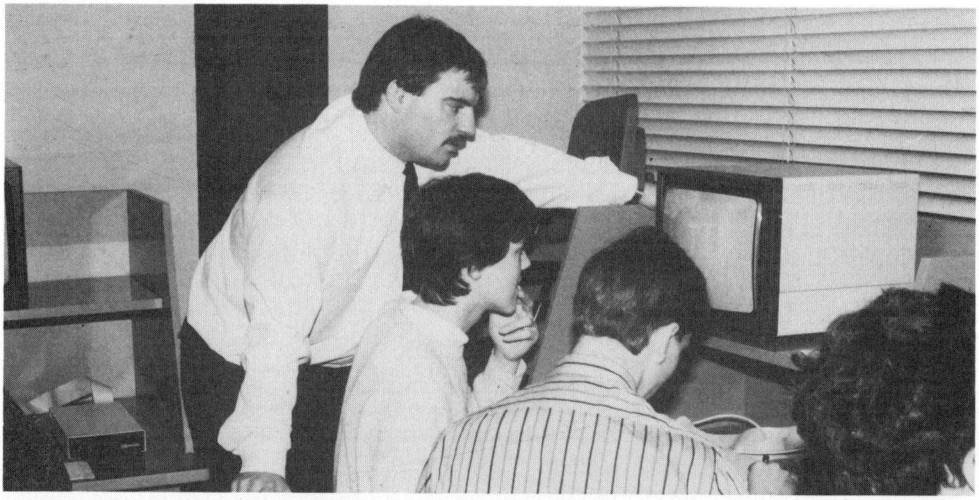

reports or articles in journals may also provide a useful 'starter' to such sessions. However, it must be said that the success of such discussions will usually hinge crucially on the manner and extent to which we in our role of leader provide the necessary stimulus. Whenever possible the session should lead to members trying some related activity in their own classrooms with the opportunity to report back at a later meeting.

iv) In-service training has an important part to play in relevant professional development. The Mathematical Association and the Association of Teachers of Mathematics have annual conferences as well as local activities. Local authorities arrange, usually through the Mathematics Advisers, local INSET and are usually receptive to suggestions for activities.

v) It is important that the necessary material resources to facilitate a rich curriculum are not only available but are *readily* available. We need to ensure that items of equipment, specialised stationery and such material as worksheets giving starting points for investigations are easily accessible when needed. This responsibility is time-consuming but is one that can often be delegated to another senior member of the department.

Written statements of curriculum policy

The written guidance provided for the teaching programme in a department should attempt to indicate not only *what* is intended to be achieved by each group of pupils but also *how* it is to be achieved. It is in this latter respect that our written guidance so often fails to give the necessary help. A conventional outline of topics to be covered is simply incapable of conveying anything of the educational thinking within which the programme was conceived. Thus a major question to be faced by any curricular planning group is how the spirit of the intention can be retained in the written description of the course. It is likely that this can best be achieved by a multi-pronged approach, perhaps drawing upon the following ideas:

i) a clear initial statement of educational philosophy and aims (as discussed in 'Planning the curriculum')

ii) a listing of the sequence of mathematics topics or activities – i.e. a syllabus – against which teachers can design their individual programmes of work

iii) guidance material providing cross-references to specific materials or equipment to assist the wide teaching approach which is intended (as considered in 'The teaching approach')

iv) specimen questions indicating the full range of intended assessment, i.e. oral, written, practical, investigative, closed or open-ended etc. It is difficult to over-stress the importance of such examples as the style of questioning so often establishes a teaching style. For example, when a 'maths in context' approach is intended, then examples of the style of question will usually be absolutely vital

v) justification for the inclusion of the topic by cross-reference to the curricular aims and objectives. This can serve the important purpose of stressing that some topics are included principally for the vital role of developing 'thinking skills'. Clearly such indication can greatly clarify the curricular intention

vi) reference to particular sections of textbooks etc. either to commend or to draw attention to a need for alternative or supplementary treatment

vii) reference to topics particularly lending themselves to co-operative teaching, use of computers etc.

viii) department-produced teaching notes, worked examples etc. for topics meriting such supplementary treatment. (However, care should be taken to avoid impression that mathematics consists of 'standard correct answers')

ix) accounts of how lessons on 'ordinary' topics can be presented in an open-ended or investigative approach

x) a (not too rigid) indication of allocation of time for topics for particular classes as part of guidance to highlight differentiated intention

xi) indication of the learning difficulties that many pupils experience with particular topics

xii) reference to the style of assessment to be adopted within the department

xiii) record of agreed strategies and notation conventions to be used in the teaching in the department.

Producing such a statement will inevitably be a cumulative process. There is much to be said for it appearing in the form of a departmental handbook which is in loose-leaf form, perhaps in a ring folder, which will readily facilitate the changes that must inevitably occur as the curriculum and the guidance material develop. Use of differently coloured sheets and some indexing may greatly assist the document's usefulness.

Monitoring implementation

Given that a department has produced a working framework for the mathematics curriculum then it will be necessary to monitor the effectiveness of that policy and in particular:

i) colleagues' understanding of the teaching scheme

ii) the adequacy of resources for teaching to the scheme

iii) the suitability of the scheme itself for the pupils for whom it is intended.

How is this to be undertaken? Probably not as a monitoring procedure in its own right but more as an integral part of liaison with all the members of the department. The best prospect of unanimity of outlook and practice within a department is likely to be achieved if those teachers, working as a body, have themselves formulated the details of content and teaching approach. The following suggestions for monitoring may be found useful:

a) sensitive awareness of, for example, informal comments in the staffroom which point to a need for discussions with individual teachers on particular issues
b) group/departmental discussions
c) joining colleagues for a degree of collaborative teaching in the classroom
d) joining colleagues in the classroom in order to consider particular aspects of curricular provision (e.g. adequacy of individualised teaching materials, strategies for engaging pupils in discussion about mathematics)
e) advocacy of appropriate INSET provision, including school-based INSET
f) regular assessment/testing of pupils ensuring adequate match of style of assessment with aspect under test
g) comments from pupils and/or parents
h) outsiders, such as advisers or other heads of maths departments can be invited into school to look at some of the work of the department and offer informal comment
i) visits to other schools to compare their practice with one's own.

Assessment

The growing mood of accountability both within and beyond schools will continue to cause us to place greater emphasis on assessment. As is pointed out in *Mathematics from 5 to 16* (pp 45):

> . . . the performance of the pupils reflects the nature of what is provided by the school and so the quality of the mathematics curriculum itself requires continuous evaluation.

Few teachers would contest the proposition that pupil assessment is an integral part of the teaching process. However, the implementation of this important aspect of teaching, be it the routine diagnostic assessment and help given to pupils as the teacher moves around the classroom or the more formal periodic tests, can range from the casual to the over-zealous.

Some teachers, particularly those first entering the profession, find it difficult to judge the right amount of marking. It is useful, within the department's written policy, to provide guidelines for the extent and also the breadth of marking. This guidance should give some impression of a desirable balance between homework, classwork, written work, oral work, practical work and more formal assessments. To quote from the 1984 DES publication *Education Observed 2* (paragraph 22):

> Much of the marking, however, is unduly concerned with overall scores and the correction of superficial errors. In those few schools which have deliberately developed a constructive and sensitive policy, marking serves to point the pupils to new possibilities or to query the judgements they have made.

Current educational trends are attaching ever increasing importance to diagnostic skills and this should prompt us to place a strong emphasis on the development of the oral skills of informal diagnosis in the classroom. The use of pupil self-assessment can provide valuable insight into many aspects of an individual pupil's thinking. Here again, we are in a strong position to lead by example while ensuring prominent reference to the matter in the departmental handbook.

It is obviously necessary for a department to have a clear structure for the more formal periodic assessments across the full age group. Such matters are likely to become of increasing importance given the adoption by GCSE examinations of a wider variety of styles of assessing attainment. The Mathematical Association booklet *Evaluation* contains much useful material on teachers' record keeping, standardised tests, and profiles.

In all these matters it is important that our own views are well thought out and that we are consequently equipped to lead our department through discussion to a written policy which takes full account of pupils' needs and at the same time is also manageable by teachers.

Appendix 2.3 gives brief details of several assessment schemes developed in the mid-eighties reflecting the curriculum implications of the Cockcroft Report and the more widespread interest in profiling e.g. the Graded Assessment in Mathematics Scheme, the SMP/Oxford and Cambridge Board Assessment Scheme and the Oxford Certificate of Educational Achievement. Proposals for national testing at the ages of 7, 11, 14 and 16 will undoubtedly reflect the experiences gained in these earlier initiatives.

The evolving curriculum

In addition to all the tasks already discussed in this chapter, we are also held responsible for on-going developments in the curriculum. Indeed we have to aim to create a climate of thinking in the department which regards such developments as both necessary and desirable. Occasionally this may require a re-think of the whole structure, more often it will involve pruning redundant material, changes of emphasis or order, grafting in new topics and approaches.

But calls for change will arise from outside our own department. How are these to be treated? Preceding any response to external developments, there is a need for (a) *awareness* of suggestions or pressures for change and (b) *judgement* on the appropriateness of the change for our situation. Keeping up to date with developments in mathematics education is therefore a priority for a HoD. The complexity of coursework as proposed by the five GCSE examining groups (usefully summarised by the *Times Educational Supplement*, and reproduced in Appendix 2.4) exemplifies how demanding this is. A short list of information and discussion providers might include:

i) briefing conferences organised by local advisers or training institutions

ii) mathematics teaching journals
iii) *Times Educational Supplement*, particularly the mathematics supplements (usually two per year)
iv) professional conferences, courses etc.

Considerably more difficult are the judgements about whether the developments are for us. In the last decade issues such as mixed ability teaching, introducing calculators, the place of imperial units of measurement, use of microcomputers, the place of investigations, and the introduction of GCSE have all confronted HoDs. A critical mind, professional links with other HoDs, training institution tutors and advisers and good communication with internal colleagues can all contribute to good decision making in respect of the validity of the change and its appropriateness for our own situation.

Departmental meetings can encourage all members of the department to consider new approaches and share their views and experiences with colleagues. Involvement of the department in national or local projects can be helpful in providing stimulus and encouraging less adventurous colleagues to try new approaches. Such involvement can often lead to a greater sense of unity and, for example, foster collaborative teaching or other examples of curriculum development.

Conclusions - in the real world

Although we wish to continue to hold fast to high ideals we are nevertheless obliged to function in the real world with all its constraints and shortcomings! It is perhaps worth stating the obvious that the curriculum in a school is essentially a compromise between aspirations and that which is possible at a given time and in particular circumstances. Thus it may happen that those with the greatest vision and the highest standards may well experience disappointment and frustration.

Often we have to try to fit our hopes and aspirations into a longer time span and appreciate that the graph of change seldom shows a positive gradient throughout. Nevertheless, we live in a world of accelerating change, and it seems unlikely that an exception of constancy will be made for mathematics education. There is the potential for both us and our colleagues in the department to develop as professionals through both the creative experiences and the problems of design and implementation. It is hoped that later chapters in this handbook will provide further useful guidance.

3 Concern with pupils

Chris Rigby is the representative pupil towards whom the whole mathematics education enterprise in our school is directed. He or she (whichever you prefer but hereafter referred to as 'she' for simplicity) is one of some 4 000 000 pupils who are our combined responsibility in the secondary schools of the UK. She has a life of her own, partly in school and partly outside. Mathematics is but a part of the former life and is probably regarded as an insignificant element in the latter. She may not rate us very important (except perhaps when a decision about an exam entry approaches) but we need to regard her as central to our concerns if our provision for all the pupils is to be appropriate and effective.

Chris may well be affected by several discontinuities in her mathematical environment. It seems important to acknowledge some of these before looking specifically at her needs:

i) between her perspective on mathematics education and ours	Her viewpoint is coloured by her experience to date, her natural ability and attainment and the perceived relevance of the subject. A challenge to us to enrich the experience, develop the ability, maximise the attainment and captivate the interest.

ii) between the school's philosophy and policy and that of the mathematics department	Our activities take place within the context of the larger framework of school. How do the two relate with respect to concern for individual pupils, e.g. views on grouping pupils, demands made on pupil time, commitment etc?
iii) between her mathematics teacher and the Head of Department	Where does our responsibility begin and end in contrast with that of our colleague whose class she is in? How does the pupil view us? What is our desired 'image' as a HoD?
iv) between herself and the whole school population	The school environment provides a vital part of the educational experience but how are the needs of the individual affected by the requirements of large teaching groups and the practical difficulties of responding to one pupil amongst many?

Having sought to identify these discontinuities and to comment briefly upon them, we will leave them to form a backdrop to all that follows.

Chris Rigby's mathematical education - the needs

It is perhaps most useful to focus on a number of specific themes.

INDUCTION

Recognising the widespread feelings of inadequacy about performance in mathematics even at the transfer from primary stage, it seems vital to give due attention to Chris's attitudes and feelings about mathematics. Few things can be more daunting than to be greeted by a battery of tests on starting secondary school. Few things can be more dispiriting than being given three or four weeks work, to brush up on the four operations on whole numbers, fractions and decimals.

Good liaison with feeder schools and a suitable programme of work for the first half term should aim to develop confidence, enthusiasm, co-operative working and communication about mathematics. What better time to present a positive and wide view of what mathematics is.

This introductory period may also be important for diagnosing particular difficulties or particular strengths. Do such qualities need particular instruments for identification? Is such information to be centrally co-ordinated?

APPROPRIATE TEACHING

Some aspects of appropriateness for Chris Rigby at various stages of secondary education might be:

i) matching her state of knowledge
ii) identifying and responding to her particular difficulties
iii) extending her to develop her potential in mathematics
iv) providing some continuity of teaching with a demonstrated interest in progress
v) developing an awareness of herself as a learner, using the teacher as a resource
vi) responding to spurts of development or slumps in interest
vii) recognising that adolescents in groups need stimulus, encouragement and some clear boundaries to achieve their best
viii) providing regular feedback on progress
ix) linking mathematics with the world outside school.

Meeting such requirements needs an excellent teacher and these are in short supply. In practice, the demands of the group, both in terms of immediate management and in learning complexity will cause many of these needs to drop below the horizon, while we as teachers recognise and wrestle with our own individual and pressing needs. Nevertheless, at times the feeling of being 'processed' in a group may be one of the most undermining elements in Chris Rigby's experience of learning mathematics.

EQUIPMENT AND RESOURCES

A checklist in the form of questions might best provide a stimulus to thought and review. What are pupils expected to provide? How is this expectation communicated? Is the expectation consistently expressed by the way members of the department operate in their classrooms?

Are there departmental resources to act as a stop gap where pupils forget, lose or cannot afford? Is it possible to obtain replacements at a within-school 'shop'?

Do resources such as textbooks have a part to play in providing structure and continuity? Is the use of workcards and small booklets together with the shortage of finance for class texts seriously weakening the response to pupil needs?

What might Chris Rigby (or her parents) reasonably expect to be spent on resources relating to her mathematics education this year?

Have pupils access to textual material in class, department or school libraries? What access is there to calculator, computer and other more expensive resources? Is there access to mathematics resources outside the school through visits, speakers, competitions?

MONITORING PROGRESS

Informal monitoring and feedback in oral work and class work provide awareness of concern and encourage pupil awareness of development. Written comments on homework, while time consuming, offer the possibility of response to the individual pupil. In tests and examinations, Chris needs to feel that the assessment of her progress is both valid and reliable (not her terms!), that the outcome is open and intelligible to her. Too often in the past pupils have been satisfied or demoralised by marks which reveal little but somehow assign a pass or fail outcome to them depending on whether or not they scored 50 or more marks! Current developments in assessment offer hope of providing feedback on more valid measures of progress.

ADVICE ON THE NEXT STAGE

At least three 'next stages' can be envisaged and are considered in turn.

i) *Moving to another school* Pupil and parents are often in need of advice as they face the educational decisions required when moving to another part of the country. Chris Rigby may need to know what kinds of course will follow on more or less naturally from the one at our school. How does SMP A-level compare with MEI or the London syllabus B? How does another GCSE group's mathematics syllabus compare with the one we use? Do we have the information or the expertise to advise? At the same time, have we the means to inform the new school about the strengths, weaknesses and stage of progress of Chris to ensure minimum disruption on moving? (What would we find it useful to know about a pupil arriving in February of the 4th year?!)

ii) *Moving to further and higher education* Chris may not be planning to study maths at university but some of her peers will. What advice might we give? What do we know about the mathematics courses at various universities and polytechnics; what are the mathematical demands of physics, engineering, economics courses? The local college of FE runs BTEC courses with all manner of specialisms; what mathematics is involved? Are there ways in which such a data bank can be established?

iii) *Getting a job* The school doubtless has a specialist careers teacher and will have the services of the LEA careers service. We need to be aware of what information is available for pupils in relation to their mathematical ability, the entry qualifications required for particular employment, what careers are linked to the study of mathematics at various levels. As a girl, Chris Rigby perhaps needs to get some of this information at an early age in order to avoid the frequently observed tendency for girls to move away from quantitative subjects too soon, with a consequent narrowing of career possibilities.

Much of the information required for giving advice seems difficult and certainly time consuming to obtain. Other schools or resource centres may have at least some of it. Some co-operative effort to improve the data base may well be fruitful. Might appropriate advice even lead to another generation of mathematics teachers?

Teaching groups

1) *CRITERIA FOR GROUPING*

Whatever the number of pupils in each year group, it is likely to require some subdivision to form acceptable teaching groups consistent with current staffing levels. In the lower school, groups of 25 to 30, each with a teacher seem normal. The way they are grouped seems likely to depend on one or more of the following:

School policy	• is there an edict from the head or an agreement by heads of department that a particular form of grouping shall be used in each of the years? • is there special provision for the least able in the form of remedial groups or a floating remedial teacher?
Depart-mental policy	• this may arise from a particular philosophy about education in general or mathematics education in particular, which has led to particular kinds of teaching and particular types of curriculum material e.g. a strong belief in mixed ability teaching for all. • it may be an attempt to enable individual staff to feel most comfortable in teaching in their own way.
The timetable	• desirable practice which is consistent with policies has to recognise the constraints of the timetable not only in appropriate lengths of lessons but in respect of teaching groups. Can eight or nine mathematics teachers be found to teach a whole year group at the same time? If not, then a year group may have been split to produce two parallel half-year groups each covering the full ability range.

While only departmental policy is within our remit, the other factors seem likely to be reviewed from time to time offering opportunities for modification.

Some determinants of the mathematics department policy may be as follows:

i) a perceived need to have changing systems of grouping across the five years, usually involving an attempt to produce increasingly narrow bands of ability within the group

ii) a wish to give pupils a fresh start in secondary school, not relying too heavily on test scores or other evidence from several feeder primary schools. (Alternatively, a desire to sort them out as quickly as possible using tests in the first week of entry!)

iii) the intention of avoiding unrealistic fine tuning of any setting system (e.g. Sets 1–13 by ability in a large school!), or the wish to set as sharply and as soon as possible

iv) a recognition that if pupil ability is *roughly* normally distributed then the ability range in highest and lowest sets is likely to be greater than that in the middle

v) a desire to enable easy movement between sets during a year

vi) an interest in the arrangements in years 4 and 5 relating appropriately to different entry levels for GCSE

vii) a belief that more able, well motivated classes can afford to be larger in size than those of less able pupils requiring more individual attention

viii) the hope of having a system which can be explained to parents and other outsiders!

2) *SOME GROUPING STRUCTURES*

i) *Grouping in Years 1 to 3* There are probably dozens of different ways exhibited by practice around the country. The three models shown in Figure 3.1(a) typify some common types of grouping practice.

——— Indicates a teaching group; commonly used terms for grouping are listed below.

Model 1

Year 1	Year 2	Year 3
———— ———— ———— ———— ———— ———— ———— ————	either as Year 1 or ———— A ———— A ———— A ———— A ———— B ———— B ———— B ———— B	———— 1 A ———— 2 A ———— 3 A ———— 4 A ———— 1 B ———— 2 B ———— 3 B ———— 4 B
Mixed ability* groups (e.g. tutor groups)	Two ability bands* within which the maths department forms mixed teaching groups	Two ability bands*, pupils set within each band

Model 2

Year 1	Year 2	Year 3
———— A ———— α ———— A ———— α ———— A ———— α ———— A ———— α	———— 1 A ———— 1 α ———— 2 A ———— 2 α ———— 3 A ———— 3 α ———— 4 A ———— 4 α	As in Year 2
Parallel half year* groups and mixed ability	Setting* within half years	

Model 3

Year 1	Year 2	Year 3
———— ———— ———— ———— ———— ———— ————	———— 1 ———— 2 ———— 3 ———— 4	As in Year 2
Seven mixed ability groups with additional float teacher timetabled to support least able pupils.	Four maths 'ability' levels, some with several mixed groups. Additional teacher allows two small groups at level 4.	

*grouping terms used

mixed ability –	a group covering the whole ability range with the possible exception of a remedial group separately catered for
bands –	broad ability groupings involving half or a third of a year group relating perhaps to attainment in general rather than in mathematics alone
parallel half-years –	a year group split into two halves each with the full ability range
setting –	grouping within a subject by attainment.

Figure 3.1(a)

ii) *Grouping in Years 4 and 5* Mathematics will generally be a core course in the teaching programme which may allow the whole year to be timetabled for mathematics simultaneously or at least in two halfyear groups. The year 3 grouping system may serve, but the need to prepare for external examinations may require some restructuring. The structure of curriculum materials which have been adopted (e.g. SMP 11–16's Yellow, Red, Blue, Green courses) may suggest particular forms of grouping. Throughout the implementation of any particular system, we need constantly to be aware of the dangerous myth that children can be neatly ranked across a year group.

Within the department, it seems likely that the level of GCSE papers to be taken, or the fact that no GCSE maths papers are to be taken, will influence thinking about grouping. While it is difficult to avoid labelling and the potential alienation of some groups of pupils, a sense of success and of the programme being valued by staff may go a long way in avoiding the most negative aspects of labelling. Even at this stage the system needs to be flexible enough to allow movement between groups.

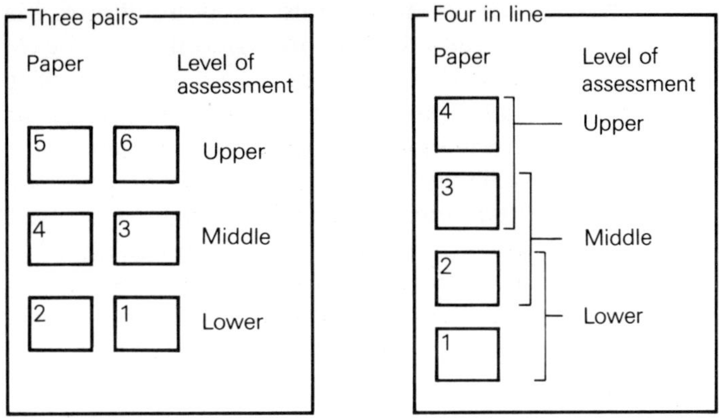

Figure 3.1(b)

Two models used by GCSE Examining Groups to achieve three levels

3) PROCEDURES FOR GROUPING

Ideally our procedures should be known and understood both by parents and pupils. In practice, it is often more comfortable to operate a system without close scrutiny from outsiders. However, while there will always be a degree of arbitrariness, we should have a defensibly rational system which recognises the affective attributes of pupils as well as the cognitive. A major re-organisation is likely if at some stage we move from mixed ability groups to setting by ability. The following seem important elements of the process:

- Ensuring that colleagues are clear about the procedure and the timing. (Is it in the departmental handbook?)

- Draft recommendations from staff recorded perhaps on a broadsheet available for scrutiny in the departmental office.
- A meeting to confirm grouping.
- Informing pupils of both the new system of grouping and their initial place in it.

4) *MOVEMENT BETWEEN SETS*

The possibility of this mobility probably features prominently in our publicity for parents but this doesn't make it straightforward. Set a test between two adjacent sets and the marks will overlap considerably. Do we change 20 per cent of the group in response to the test scores or resort to a football league approach – three up, three down, or have we a more professionally sophisticated and defensible method? Our approach may largely depend on the department's approach to assessment and on the kinds of communication possible between the teachers of adjacent sets. Unless the outcome is the status quo, we shall have to deal with both the promoted and demoted.

Do promoted pupils need additional teaching to cover work not previously done or are we confident they will cope on elation? How can demoted pupils be prevented from dropping further through the system, particularly if poor motivation was the root cause of poor performance? Have we any evidence in the department about the mobility of pupils in the ability groups over five years? Are we simply responding to genuine change in rates of mathematical development or are we promoting it by our procedures? What is evident is that most mathematics teachers have enjoyed the motivating atmosphere of being near the top of the system! Perhaps all our systems need scrutiny for the hidden messages which they carry.

Particular needs

Although we started the chapter focussing on the needs of the individual pupil, it is helpful in thinking about appropriate provision to recognise clusters of particular needs. In recent years increasing attention has been given to the particular needs of low attainers, of girls, of ethnic minorities, of high achievers and of those with 'special educational needs'. This handbook is not the place to discuss each of these in detail but a brief consideration of issues together with reference to recent publications (see Appendix 7 'Sources and resources') will hopefully be of value.

GIRLS AND MATHEMATICS

The concern in this area undoubtedly reflects a major movement during the seventies and eighties towards equal opportunities and the removal of gender bias in many different fields. The mathematics education world has developed its own pressure group to address the problems typified by the data which appears in the Royal Society's report *Girls and Mathematics*.

Performance of females and males in O-level Mathematics (1985)*
(47.3% of total entry is female)

	Grades				
	A	B	C	D	E
Males	63.6	56.8	52.0	48.6	47.8
Females	36.4	43.2	48.0	51.4	52.2

Performance of females and males in A-level (pure and applied) Mathematics (1984)*
(30.3% of total entry is female)

	Grades				
	A	B	C	D	E
Males	75.0	69.8	69.0	66.0	66.7
Females	25.0	30.2	31.0	34.0	33.3

*Percentage of males and females awarded each grade is given.

Over and above any pervading movement for 'equality', there is rightful concern about girls apparently rejecting educational opportunities in mathematics when the country is so short of people qualified in mathematics at many levels. However, as with many educational issues there are few simple, agreed explanations and even fewer agreed strategies for solution.

On the cognitive side, the outcome of various studies (particularly the APU) suggests that:

i) up to twelve plus there is no statistically significant sex difference in average mathematics scores; differences occur in the types of item successfully dealt with by each sex
M. Eddowes, *Humble Pi: the Mathematics Education of Girls* (Longman for Schools Council, 1983)

ii) boys are significantly better on test items requiring 'spatial ability'
iii) boys are better at more complex items requiring abstract thought, problem solving, breaking set (e.g. using non standard methods), conceptualisation
iv) girls are better at simple repetitive tasks requiring low-level skills such as rule following
R. Walden and V. Walkerdine, *Girls and Mathematics* (University of London Institute of Education, 1985)

Many believe, however, that attitudes play a much more significant role in the outcome. Attitudes to mathematics are found to become less positive with age; the deterioration is more marked for girls than boys. Girls' confidence in themselves mathematically and their expectations of success are less than those of boys. Walden and Walkerdine see the problems centred in a 'tortuous and contradictory relationship between gender (masculinity/femininity) and intellectuality (academic performance and attainment)'. The perceived feminine characteristics of being 'helpful', 'nice', 'kind' and 'attractive' are claimed to help render the girls 'good and hardworking in the classroom and so lead to academic success, but not to a display of those characteristics which are read as indicating "real understanding", "flair", "brilliance" and so forth'.

Suggestions for action

i) *Raise level of awareness of issues with colleagues – perhaps at a departmental meeting.*

ii) *Consider the situation in your own school by looking at for example*
   - a) *entries for GCE A-level*
   - b) *performance in internal exams, proportion of girls in sets changes occurring over the 11–16 range.*

iii) *Consider whether sex bias is prevalent in*
   - a) *listing, grouping pupils*
   - b) *teacher interactions in the classrooms; boys in general get more attention from the teacher – use of teacher observers?*
   - c) *syllabus content – is adequate time allowed to overcome differential success in particular parts of the curriculum (e.g. spatial work)?*
   - d) *curriculum materials e.g. showing girls only in feminine role or centering only on pursuits of more interest to boys*
   - e) *teacher expectations of girls' performance*
   - f) *implicit messages to pupils and parents about careers suitable for girls. (Do we have a responsibility to be more active in communicating the importance of mathematics in careers?)*

iv) *Monitor progress and developments in this field over several years. Changes in attitudes and performance will not happen quickly. Evidence of slow but definite change should encourage us.*

Advice given to Heads of Department by the Royal Society Report is reproduced in Appendix 3.1.

ETHNIC MINORITY GROUPS

Our concern as HoDs about this issue seems likely to reflect the prevalence of such groups in our own school. If they are absent or very few in number we may be inclined to ignore the issue. (Educationalists energetically concerned with preparing chidren for a multi-cultural society might well claim we were consequently one of the major hindrances to progress!) Those HoDs with a substantial proportion of pupils from such minority groups may be aware of curricular responses from the English, history and other departments but see the international language of mathematics to be above such a need for change. Until recently, relatively little has been published in this field but an article by Derek Woodrow in the *TES* Mathematics Supplement of May 1984 makes for thoughtful reading. Some of the points raised are summarised below.

It is suggested that introducing Islamic geometrical patterns and bits of history relating to mathematics in other cultures, may be simply irrelevant tokenism. Nevertheless attempts to show mathematics as an international tool and to place applications in a not too narrow cultural context are to be welcomed. The real problems for ethnic minority groups in mathematics may lie in other directions, for example:

i) Languages differ considerably in their adequacy for making distinctions between mathematical concepts e.g. a language using the same word for 'small' and 'few', and only having one word for 'round' and 'circle'. A frequently used mother tongue may inhibit the development of certain concepts.
ii) Visualing and interpreting diagrams is strongly influenced by cultural experiences. (This is well documented, for example, in many developing countries.) Mathematics teaching relies heavily on the development and use of such skills.
iii) Psychological differences may be evident in the match between the approved style of behaviour in a culture and the way mathematics is taught. Being right or wrong creates different problems in different cultures. An authoritarian, self-disciplined, group-dependent society in which individuality is suppressed creates attitudes sympathetic to a 'traditional' approach to mathematics teaching. A more restive, exuberant culture may be less supportive to common approaches to mathematics learning.

The claim that school mathematics is culture-free has as little validity as the claim made by a sophisticated person that she doesn't have an accent. The increasing emphasis on 'mathematics in context' makes the cultural base more explicit. (How do we respond to statistics questions on baseball or probability questions on freedom fighters?) The issues relating to the process of teaching and the nature of the activities involved in learning mathematics are more subtle but are almost certainly even more important.

Suggestions for action

i) Raising the level of awareness of the issue and some of its dimensions with members of the department.
ii) Raising the level of awareness of our own racial prejudice as teachers as a starting point for working towards the removal of racism from the mathematics curriculum. In particular, avoiding the use of resources which show different cultures in outdated stereotyped roles.
iii) Explore, perhaps with language colleagues, particular linguistic and other cultural influences which may affect the mathematics education of minorities present in our school.

iv) If necessary, study more closely the additional support which may be needed by some pupils in the face, for example, of more open-ended kinds of work. (A task for your colleagues studying for an MEd?)

v) Enrich the curriculum with a view of mathematics developing within cultures. Counting and numeration systems, measurement systems, computational devices, types of pattern and geometrical design all make for interesting and worthwhile study.

PUPILS WITH SPECIAL NEEDS

The proposals of the Warnock Report have caused considerable discussion and some action relating to pupils with particular needs. Their statement to the effect that 'at any one time one child in six is likely to require some form of special educational provision' challenges the prevalent view that the special schools cope with the special needs problem. The magnitude of the population with special needs together with the closer integration of pupils with physical handicaps have caused schools to review provision. As far as we are aware there are few studies and little specific advice for responding to this newly preceived situation in mathematics. The importance of awareness, diagnosis and appropriate strategies for meeting needs is easy to state but is likely to be difficult to execute, with the certain demand on time and probable need for skills which may not be well developed. In the suggestions which follow the needs of the 'low attainers', or of the 'gifted', are not discussed since these are considered in later sections.

Suggestions for action

i) The department might usefully draw up a list of special needs
- *pupils who have a period or periods of prolonged absence*
- *pupils who show rapidly changing levels of performance – positive or negative change*
- *pupils entering the system from a different school*
- *pupils with a strikingly different level of achievement in say maths and English or, perhaps between problem-solving ability and psychomotor ability, or between mental and written work*
- *pupils with visual or hearing impairment etc.*

ii) Members of staff might identify pupils in the above categories from those classes which they are currently teaching. Do they have the means to identify them?

iii) Can appropriate action or resource support be identified and provided (e.g. if there are pupils in wheelchairs, is particular equipment necessary to meet their needs? Can they follow an identical curriculum with their peers without additional support? Is additional adult help available as pupils with more severe needs are integrated into schools? Is there a need for an after-school or lunch time 'clinic' for those who have missed work?)

iv) Consultation with other departments and with those with pastoral responsibilities together with monitoring activity over a period of time may allow progress to be identified and maintained.

LOW ATTAINERS

While the other three categories of particular needs may be well camouflaged, we are all acutely conscious of a problem in providing appropriately for low attainers, which isn't to say that many HoDs would claim that they have found the complete answer! Indeed this is the group that the student teacher is sometimes told he can do what he likes with, which presumably means the department has no clear idea of what is appropriate rather than believing that a beginner is likely to have a ready made solution!

Low attainers have for a long time been at the bottom end of the dilution process in the 'top down' approach to curriculum. Cockcroft's suggestion of a 'bottom up' curriculum has given a fresh round of impetus to thinking about the needs of low attainers. The Foundation List was an attempt to define appropriate curriculum content. Materials ranging from basic skills workbooks to activity-based materials consistent with paragraph 243's six kinds of experience continue to hit the market. Yet, the problem of meeting the needs of low attainers seems likely to persist since the complexity of the causes of low attainment is poorly matched by the resources and skills needed in the normal school setting.

The Schools Council Working Paper No. 72 *Low Attainers in Mathematics 5 to 16* explains the preference of the team of researchers for the term 'low attainers' (rather than remedial, less able, slow learner, disadvantaged, etc.) in terms of its description of observable performance without the implication of a cause. The following non-exclusive categories were suggested:

> physical, physiological or sensory defects, emotional or behavioural problems;
> impaired performance due to physical causes, such as tiredness, drugs, general ill-health;
> attitude, anxiety, lack of motivation;
> inappropriate teaching;
> too many changes of teachers, lack of continuity;
> general slowness in grasping ideas;
> cultural differences, English not first language;
> impoverished home background;
> difficulty in oral expression or in written work, poor reading ability;
> gaps in education, absence from school, frequent transfer from one school to another;
> immaturity, late development, youngest in the year group;
> low self-concept leading to lack of self-confidence.

The report goes on to analyse causes into three categories, those beyond the control of the school, those partly within the control of the school and those wholly within the control of the school.

While every school has its lowest attainers, the actual proportion of low attainers (defined say as the lowest 20 per cent nationally) may vary between 2 or 3 per cent and perhaps 40 per cent depending on the school's catchment area. Responses by school and department to situations within this range must be very different.

Suggestions for action

i) *Review current prevalence of and provision for low attainers in the school and department. How integrated are these two levels of provision? (e.g. does a special needs teacher look after mathematics along with other subjects? What kind of communication is there between departments?)*

ii) *What kind of status does work with low attainers have in the department? What kind of resources are devoted to it – both in quantity and nature? (e.g. are practical materials available for appropriate practical work?)*

iii) *Is there a need for a specialist co-ordinator of such work in the department? Could that person be most effective by working alongside other members of the department while providing additional help for particular pupils? Will that person benefit from attending an appropriate in-service course?*

iv) *What form of in-service training within the school can help all staff develop their skills further?*

v) *What form of local advice/support is available – at a teachers' centre, from an advisory teacher?*

vi) *Review the curriculum in terms of the content (Does it go beyond computation? Are topics developed to a point where pupils see some purpose?) and the teaching approach (Is class teaching appropriate? What is the place of practical work projects?).*

vii) *Establish a resource bank of appropriate materials and a library of ideas and case studies. (See references in Appendix 7.)*

EXCEPTIONALLY ABLE PUPILS

Problems of definition are also evident with this group. Are we concerned with the top 2 per cent or the top 0.2 per cent? If this is a definition related to national ability, what are the implications for our own school which may have a skewed ability distribution as a result of the catchment area or a creaming by selective schools? If we restrict ourselves to the smaller percentage then it is likely that many schools will only have such a pupil very occasionally. The other figure corresponds roughly to those who might be expected to get an A or B at A-level. While exceptionally able pupils may not necessarily achieve these grades it perhaps forms a more realistic target group for which to plan a strategy. Amongst such a group we shall need to be prepared for the needs of the rare highly gifted pupil.

The fact that they are a minority at one extreme of the ability range immediately suggests that the normal provision within the school maths curriculum is unlikely to tax them. Regrettably this may lead them to be unnoticed as exceptionally able or may result in behavioural problems which arise from boredom and frustration. Particularly perplexing are those who may exhibit limited ability in linguistic and communication skills which thereby camouflage exceptional mathematical ability. The argument for appropriate provision is strong both at a personal and at a social level. The former is true for all pupils, the latter is of crucial importance in harnessing such unusual talent in a field where there seems almost unlimited demand.

Such exceptional ability is not of a single type. It may have shown itself early as an interest in and ability with numbers. Such pupils may learn and grasp new ideas quickly and understand abstract concepts easily; they may handle abstract concepts with ease and be able to apply them in a variety of situations. They may show strengths in particular areas of mathematics – spatial rather than algebraic say. They may show unusual energy and perseverance in pursuing ideas.

Anita Straker in her review *Mathematics for the Gifted Pupil* (1982) advocates that the school curriculum should be designed to enable ability to show and to flourish. Discussion time may be a vital method of diagnosis. She reports the use of check lists to help in identifying such pupils. Some other behavioural characteristics noted by teachers which mathematically able pupils may display, include:

- Persistence in a search for the best and simplest solution to a problem. Children who have a gift for mathematics do not easily tire when they are occupied with it. Eleven- or twelve-year-old pupils, for example, can work continuously for up to three hours before showing any deterioration in their performance.

- Self-confidence in a new mathematical situation, where they are prepared to use initiative in tackling something different. They make statements like: 'I know, I'll try so and so', or 'No, that can't be right because . . .', or 'Look, I'll show you'.

- Open-mindedness in that mathematically capable children will weigh evidence, and be prepared to change a point of view according to the evidence.

- Perpetual posing of problems to themselves, during lessons and at home: 'How many people could stand on the Wembley football pitch?', 'How many seconds does a person live in a lifetime?', 'What area can you see from the top of the GPO Tower?', 'How fast is that aeroplane going?', etc.

- Terse, even laconic, expression of thought. This may show itself in mathematics where there may be a dislike in the early stages of writing out solutions to problems which can be solved mentally, but also in written work in English.

Whatever the form of school and classroom organisation, the talents of the gifted in mathematics can only be matched if staff are sensitive to their needs and have the ideas and resources to respond. Encouraging independence in study and being able to provide appropriate materials seems vital.

Suggestions for action

i) *Consider with colleagues how individual needs can be met within the teaching of the general programme. Is it possible to identify such pupils with the course materials currently used?*

ii) *Review the incidence of high ability in mathematics in pupils at your school. Review provision made for them – are special demands made, are there special resources available, is it a matter of staff concern that their talent should be developed?*

iii) *Develop a bank of special resources. The Schools Council guide prepared by Anita Straker has a good starting list.*

iv) *Look for opportunities beyond the school both to extend the very able and to give them contact with other able pupils, for example*

   a) *mathematical competitions – the National Mathematical Contest etc.*

   b) *responding to problems and puzzles in magazines e.g.* Mathematical Spectrum *or writing articles for mathematical magazines e.g.* Hypotenuse, Plus

   c) *courses, clubs organised by LEAs, local colleges of higher education or universities. If they don't exist in the area, could a group of schools sponsor some such activity?*

   d) *'masterclasses' if they are held in the area? If not, might something be arranged?*

Conclusion

Responding day by day to the needs of individual pupils seems an almost impossible task in the face of the pressure of class units of 30 pupils. It is important then, to develop strategies for making appropriate responses. Concerted efforts to work on the needs of particular groups followed by a system of monitoring should enable significant progress to be made. Giving particular staff members responsibility for an area may well be the most effective strategy and may preserve the life and sanity of the HoD for other aspects of his or her work!

4 Concern with colleagues

For most of us the first months of being a HoD produced an acute awareness of the dramatic change of role which affected our lives. We were now held responsible for the mathematical education of all pupils and not just those in our own classes, but we could only exercise that responsibility through our colleagues. This required a major change of perspective with an immediate need for appropriate management skills.

We had felt ourselves to be competent and confident teachers ready for promotion, committed and involved in helping to develop the mathematics curriculum and in administering the departments to which we belonged. Short courses had allowed us to familiarise ourselves with current developments and to try out ideas in discussion. Some of us had been able to take part in longer management courses and thereby felt rather better prepared, but all of us had at least been able to convince an appointments panel of our potential to become an effective Head of Department.

Our 'clear' views of the leadership role based upon personality and philosophy had to be modified and broadened rapidly as we worked through the variety of new situations presented daily in our schools. We had to be involved in leading whilst learning, and assisting whilst monitoring. A taxing and sometimes distressing role, as we related the strengths and inadequacies of ourselves and others with the needs of pupils and the demands of a constantly shifting set of expectations and demands from outside; the GCSE system and the emphasis on vocational relevance being current examples. In this chapter we concentrate on our task of managing the team of mathematics teachers. We shall do this under the following headings:

What type of leader?
Handling diversity in the departmental team
Appointing staff
Professional development
Career progression.

What type of leader?

On appointment we are almost certainly the outsider – the last one in. We are responsible for a group 'gathered' over the years by others. They still bear the imprint of our predecessors and are waiting with interest and perhaps apprehension for us to show our colours. Two very distinct strategies are easily described. Start as we mean to go on, by presenting a bold plan for action to achieve the implemented radical curriculum. Or the softly-softly approach – get to know the situation and the staff first, no changes for at least a term, then by stages, with staff participation, move towards implementing the identified curriculum. The first strategy may seem consistent with the bold statements made at interview. It demands confidence bordering on arrogance, raising significant issues about our views of colleagues as professionals. The second approach appears to give greater respect for the judgements of colleagues (and predecessors?) but might it miss a golden opportunity for change when the constraints are at a minimum?

In practice we are not likely to operate at either extreme but can doubtless identify colleagues who were close to the models described! Our temperament may immediately incline us to one model rather than the other, but an awareness of this trait should probably be an encouragment to caution. What seems to be vital is that we make a leadership style explicit. The indicators which follow could be a way of doing this in support of a particular style:

i) a willingness to listen to colleagues' concerns about their work
ii) consulting staff in an effort to understand and to question why things are as they are
iii) providing practical support for individual colleagues when they need it (e.g. that 'impossible' blackboard with which they have struggled for years)
iv) showing a willingness to take decisions (e.g. in contacting the parents of an under-achieving pupil, supporting a colleague's application for an in-service secondment)
v) expecting professionalism from colleagues (e.g. in exercising responsibility which has been delegated).

Many such early indicators are likely to be long term characteristics of a style, but gradually more fundamental change has to occur. Awareness of substantial weaknesses in the curriculum by members of the department may make it relatively easy to consider and to agree change. At other times, our convictions and those of the department may seem at odds and it will be a far more lonely and difficult task to achieve what we believe is needed. Understanding the strengths and weaknesses of the individuals making up the team and awareness of the relationship existing between them are likely to be important determinants of success.

(Further ideas on the personal characteristics of managers are given in Appendix 4.1.)

Handling diversity in the departmental team

Many of us may feel that our departments contain a greater diversity of staff than others in the school, not simply because of the size of the department but because of the chronic problems of recruiting mathematically qualified teachers. Whilst it was hoped that the falling secondary school rolls of the late eighties might reduce the shortage, current experience indicates an increasing crisis as the demand for mathematics graduates exceeds supply and the proportion entering teaching decreases. There seems little chance, despite recent DES initiatives, that the situation will improve in the medium term future, particularly with the prospect of school rolls increasing again in the early nineties. The challenge to the Head of Mathematics therefore remains that of attempting to realise the strength bound up in diversity, whilst minimising its weaknesses.

In this context, it seems unhelpful to attempt to classify staff according to their mathematical qualifications because apart from determining who should teach the advanced courses, it has little relevance to the day to day running of the department. The following list identifies those who were most commonly mentioned as needing special consideration:

Senior colleagues
Probationary teachers
Redeployed teachers
Part-time teachers
Supply teachers
Student teachers
Teachers of pupils with special needs.

1) *SENIOR COLLEAGUES*

Clearly there are potential advantages if one of the school management team is a member of the department: information can flow more freely in both directions, direct assistance in discipline may be available and we would have an experienced colleague able to give advice directly relevant to the circumstances of the department.

A senior colleague may be able to help a new HoD gain confidence in dealing with pupils and with staff. However there can be difficulty in establishing a really good working relationship, since some may rarely contribute to departmental discussions or conversely they may so dominate discussion that they discourage others from taking part. The overlapping responsibility structures within a school cause problems for everyone and some senior staff find difficulty in playing a full part, especially in a democratically organised department numerically dominated by younger and less experienced staff.

Since pressure of other commitments can often prevent regular attendance at departmental meetings, special efforts have to be made to keep such colleagues in close contact with the work of the department. Ensuring that everyone contributes fully to departmental discussions and that no one dominates, is a problem not solely related to the presence of senior colleagues. We may well feel intimidated by some colleagues, particularly in the early months of joining the department. They may seem intelligent and articulate or perhaps argumentative and personal in their criticisms. We need to handle their contribution fairly, to recognise that their approach may arise from grudge or insecurity (best handled outside a meeting). Above all, enable other members of the group to express their views. Preliminary discussions of contentious topics with dominating colleagues can help to reduce oppressive intervention and whilst direct appeals can bring forth the views of the more reluctant, they will usually respond better if given time to prepare their contribution.

2) *PROBATIONARY TEACHERS*

The energy and enthusiasm of the new probationary teacher is usually most welcome but the professional support that must be offered is a major responsibility.

While in many schools a senior member of staff is given responsibility for all probationary teachers much of the assistance and guidance needed can only be given from within the department. Inevitably probationers come in all shapes and forms. The majority have come directly from some 17 years continuous 'processing' by the education system; a few will be mature entrants with experience as responsible employees or parents. Some may appear overconfident and dismissive of the complexities of the job, while many will feel somewhat in awe of the task they have undertaken. All need individual handling involving reassurance and support towards becoming a fully professional teacher. However it is an irresponsible profession which believes new entrants should carry the load and work with the efficiency of the experienced member. All too often this appears to be the case in teaching, with a consequent lowering of standards and an unreasonable pressure on probationers. A check list of ideas/suggestions for HoDs may be of value.

i) A somewhat reduced timetable
   - to ensure more careful preparation
   - to allow opportunities to work alongside other teachers and discuss teaching/learning with them
   - to see other subjects being taught.

ii) A weekly/fortnightly tutorial, of say 30–40 minutes, with the HoD, to talk about work in progress and to be introduced to elements of the department's work. The development of skills and appraisal, culminating in a report and the decision on granting full recognition as a teacher, should happen within this framework.

iii) Ensure that proper support is being provided for additional activities undertaken
   - pastoral work with its administrative demands
   - cover for absent colleagues when the normal shields of knowledge and preparation may not be there
   - extra mural activities – are these helping or are they simply increasing the load?

iv) A mentor who is closer in age and experience to the probationer may provide support of a kind which a HoD or deputy head may find difficult to provide. Problems regarding responsibility and confidence which may arise with a probationer having major problems need to be anticipated.

v) Avoid being misled by fake indicators. Quiet classrooms don't necessarily indicate ideal teaching and learning – or the opposite! A probationer in difficulties may still try to hide the real problems in spite of our good intentions and supportive interest.

vi) Encourage the newcomer to feel part of the team by making it clear that they have something to contribute to the life of the department – it may be in terms of ideas, knowledge of resources or taking on some small responsibility in the department.

vii) Encourage the probationer to be creative, to search out resources and to be involved in professional activity beyond the school – membership of ATM or MA, local meetings of branches etc.

viii) Provide some feedback to the training institution from which they came. Apart from news of their progress, comments on particular strengths and weaknesses which apparently relate to their training could be most useful.

3) *REDEPLOYED TEACHERS*

Most local education authorities have now established redeployment procedures as a means of coping with staffing problems associated with falling school rolls. The emphasis is usually on counselling and consent rather than on obligatory moves. Some authorities assist the process of change by guaranteeing that the teacher may return to his old school or be further redeployed if the new school is inappropriate. Since the new school accepts redeployed teachers on the same understanding, both parties can take a more relaxed stance and a successful transfer becomes more likely. In spite of all this, the trusting relationship created by the normal appointment procedure is missing and the redeployed colleagues may need much reassurance if they are to be helped through the period of uncertainty and depression associated with being 'chosen' for redeployment.

As HoDs, we might find ourselves at different times as exporters or importers. We may be in a position to offer most help to colleagues leaving our schools if we are able to ensure that the choice of which colleagues should go arises out of a positive consideration of who would most benefit from a broadened experience, rather than of which colleagues would be least missed. Under such a system both our colleagues and the new schools would have more confidence in the arrangement but in a time of increased competition between schools, it is perhaps unrealistic to expect such altruism. We may therefore in many cases only be able to offer encouragement, relying on the local authority advisers to ensure a reasonable outcome from a difficult situation. HoDs may well be able to contact their opposite numbers in the receiving schools, but in practice issues of confidence often mean that the destination of the leaving teachers is not known until almost the day of transfer.

Receiving redeployed teachers presents different challenges. While in some areas only a few mathematics teachers have so far been redeployed, experience in other departments suggests that most teachers settle more quickly and make a greater contribution if they are reassured from the outset that their presence is seen as an asset. Making a special effort to seek their views and making use of their experience is one way in which we can help them to transfer their commitment to our departments, feeling that their status is assured. All schools need a frequent influx of new ideas and the arrival of colleagues, either redeployed or perhaps returning from a period of redeployment in another school, should prove an invaluable resource. All of us need to feel valued members of our school communities if we are to give of our best.

4) *PART-TIME TEACHERS*

While often giving far more than that for which they are paid, part-time teachers often feel left out of policy making and may regard themselves as inferior members of the department. Their timetables may mean that they are not present at departmental or staff meetings and they are therefore the more dependent on written communications and minutes. The early appearance of an agenda offers an opportunity for the teacher to contribute to discussion, albeit by proxy, but fairly frequent, informal approaches are effective ways of attaching the teacher to the team.

Teachers shared between departments can also be considered in this context although they have special problems especially if both departments go out of their way to treat them as full members of their teaching team. Helping them to feel fully part of the mathematics team without making unreasonable demands upon their time and commitment is particularly difficult.

Negotiating an agreement between the teacher and the other head of department covering such matters as attendance at meetings, preparation and marking of internal examinations, can be a useful way of minimising friction. Leaving it to the hapless teacher to strike the right balance often results not only in difficulties for the teacher but in friction between the departments concerned, especially when there are tight deadlines. The shared teacher used formally as a communication link between the departments concerned may be able to make a uniquely useful contribution to the department.

5) *SUPPLY STAFF*

Arriving for occasional days or, if they are lucky, for periods of a few days or perhaps weeks, supply staff find great difficulty in offering a professional commitment even if they are mathematically qualified. They will need some specific information about the classes that they are expected to teach but it will only be those on semi-permanent supply who are likely to go through the induction process involving detailed information about the department and about the school. Since many supply teachers return to the same school on many occasions and some eventually join the school as full-time members of staff, the induction process may well not be wasted!

6) *STUDENT TEACHERS*

Student teachers usually consider teaching practice the most important component of their training and not unnaturally are very keen to work in a 'good' department in a 'good' school. We are correspondingly concerned to receive good students, whose ideas are close enough to our own to enable us to give them the greatest professional advantage whilst minimising disruption for our pupils and staff. To maximise the benefits of the practice, the following suggestions are made:

i) Obtain some background information from the institution about the course structure and content.

ii) Clarify with tutors what is expected of teaching practice in terms of:
   - amount of teaching
   - types of class
   - other kinds of experience seen as desirable
   - observation by teachers and tutors.

iii) Try to meet the students before finalising a teaching practice timetable.

iv) If it is a first major teaching practice, arrange for a gradual increase in teaching load. There are many professionally relevant activities which can be more useful than just full class teaching (e.g. thorough preparation and review of lessons, team teaching, working with small groups and individuals to provide opportunities to discover how pupils think in tackling mathematics, conversations with experienced teachers, preparing resources). While we need to feel confident at the end of a major practice that the students are able to carry a normal load in a first appointment, it is vital not to force them into hand to mouth survival on a treadmill existence at this stage.

v) Clarify purpose and practice with colleagues whose class the student will take in relation to:
   - staying in the classroom with students
   - providing opportunities for discussion about content of lessons and progress of pupils
   - providing feedback to the students (what is likely to be most helpful, at what stage?)

vi) Try to avoid rapid judgements on performance and potential. Encourage them in relation to their strengths; identify and work on weaknesses.

vii) Timetable a weekly meeting with the students to talk with you about their work. Try to identify some specific targets for their attention and for you and your colleagues' support over the next week.

viii) Provide opportunities for the students to find themselves as teachers. They may all too easily be trying to ape the five teachers whose classes they are teaching! Their first appointment may be in a department very different from yours.

ix) Make the most of their enthusiasm, energy and ideas.
x) Remember that the practice is probably intended to give students a wide experience of a teacher's work - pastoral tasks, extra-curricular activities, perhaps a subsidiary teaching subject.
xi) Keep in touch with the training institution tutors in relation to progress, potential and, of course, problems.

Most students are quick to fit into the department and value being treated as one of the team. Indeed it is this factor that leads us to conclude that the best way to treat students, when planning the practice, when giving help and advice and when assessing success, is as though they are going to join the department at the end of the practice. (Appendix 4.2 gives notes provided for staff, students and training institutions at Hartcliff School, Bristol.)

7) TEACHERS OF PUPILS WITH SPECIAL NEEDS

The links between the mathematics department and the teachers concerned with special needs vary widely from school to school: in some a member of the department has responsibility in this area whilst in others a fully autonomous department may exist with either a permanent group of pupils or a varying group withdrawn from specific lessons.

When a separate department for special needs exists, it is unusual to find mathematics teachers within it, so that an extra effort has to be made if liaison is to be adequate. It is by no means easy to maintain a programme of liaison activities over a number of years, even though everyone will agree as to its value. Working together on a common project (for example, work on 'the bottom up curriculum', or on other topics which rely equally on the different teaching skills of the two groups) seems to have greatest potential for worthwhile outcomes.

In conclusion, perhaps the main point to be recognised is that everyone working in the mathematics team has a unique and useful contribution to make and each gives most when sure that their work is valued. The diversity of the teaching staff within the department gives scope for a breadth of view of the role of mathematics that is essential if it is to make its vital contribution to the school curriculum.

Appointing staff

There are several stages in the process of appointing a new teacher to the department. In practice, the HoD may have a minority role, the initiatives being taken by the Head, who may have well established procedures for dealing with new appointments. Nevertheless, it seems important for the HoD to have thought through the process; the standard procedures may thereby be improved. After all, we shall have to work most closely with the person appointed! The various stages of the process are discussed in some detail in what follows:

Review departmental needs
Prepare a job specification
Advertise the post
Shortlist the applicants
Interview the candidates
Close the proceedings.

1) *REVIEW DEPARTMENTAL NEEDS*

Much depends upon whether a colleague is to be replaced or whether the department is expanding but in any event discussion with the Head is likely to clarify the best way forward. It appears that some heads are reluctant to discuss appointments fully, but most of us have found a more professional expectation. Clearly, this is an ideal time to consider the professional development of all members of the department, to see what gaps in the organisation of the department can be filled from within, either from existing expertise or from further training.

The most difficult task is finding the correct balance between concentrating on developing the skills of those within the department, accepting sometimes a delay before full competence is reached, and attempting to import skills and experience. The review process usually requires discussion with members of the department and problems can arise if false hopes are raised through insufficient tact and diplomacy.

It is often very difficult to replace the mixture of skills and experience that a leaving colleague has contributed to the department. The review will usually have revealed new areas into which the department needs to move and new staff may sometimes be found with the special skills and interests which are needed to stimulate change.

2) *PREPARE A JOB SPECIFICATION*

Out of the review will emerge the outline of a job specification. At times of an extreme shortage of able candidates, it is considered by many to be foolhardy to send out a very precise job specification, but others insist that suitable candidates will be more impressed by a school that has thought through its needs, and are more likely to apply. It cannot help anyone to cause candidates to waste time and money in applying for a job for which they are unsuitable.

The outline job description can then become a document to be sent to applicants along with details of the department and the school. (Appendix 4.3 provides two examples of job specifications.)

3) *ADVERTISE THE POST*

Each local education authority will have developed its own practice which may involve two or more stages. In times of re-deployment, advertising within the authority may precede a national advertisement. The style of advertisement in the *TES* is probably determined by the LEA; they may allow single adverts or may organise all their adverts into a single block. However, it is usually possible to give some 'flavour' of the school and department, mentioning special facilities or projects, even if details of the post cannot be given. The purpose is once more to encourage suitable applications and to save everyone else's time and money.

4) *SHORTLIST THE APPLICANTS*

This is another task which one would expect a Head to share with the Head of Department. However, the Head may well have requirements of the candidates beyond those of the department, and will also have a greater experience of judging the merits of the applicant from forms and letters of application. However the needs of the department must be of a high priority. Initially, it may be useful to categorise applicants as 'very suitable', 'possible', or 'unsuitable'. This would make clear our preferences in the hope that they will make an agreed short list. Under favourable circumstances a short list of five or six is appropriate.

5) *INTERVIEW THE CANDIDATES*

For mathematics appointments, interviews can rarely be treated as a simple selection process; the chosen candidate may decide not to accept the post which is offered. This advantage which a good mathematics teacher has in a shortage situation has to be borne in mind.

Selection procedures are a fairly demanding experience for most candidates and we need to keep this in mind in planning various selection activities. The invitation letter should make clear how long the candidate may be expected to spend at the school and if possible give an outline of the day's proceedings. The candidates can be expected to need a great deal of information if they are to make a rational decision. However, it is almost impossible to give detailed information while assessing the candidates at a formal interview. Delegating the task to one or two members of the department has been found very useful especially as it enables the candidates to relax at a little distance from those who will make the appointment! Whilst we may go out of our way to present a true picture of life in the department, most candidates prefer also to hear the unofficial views of teachers and pupils. We need to gain a broad impression in order to judge whether they can work in the school.

With increasing attention being given to management procedures in schools, a variety of other activities may be thought helpful in making an appointment. Those being considered may be asked to do one or more of the following:

- teach a class of pupils
- discuss their solutions to some A-level questions
- engage in group discussion or decision making with other applicants.

Individual informal interviews are a good way of discussing with candidates how they might fit into the department. At this time it is possible to gain a fairly good idea of the particular strengths and weaknesses of the candidates. The candidates will be under great pressure to give of their best and it is possible that the first impressions you are gaining are unreliable. We have all seen the consequences of poor appointments; many of these are made when personality factors are allowed to dominate other considerations. We should expect to be present at the formal interview but if local practice prevents this, we need to ensure that our reactions to each candidate, plus a ranked list of possible appointees are given to the Head. This briefing should be as detailed as possible, since a good informal interview does not guarantee a similar performance in the crucial formal interviews.

Participation as a member of an interviewing panel is often a fascinating experience – as observer of one's colleagues' interviewing technique as much as close watcher of the performance of candidates! A good chairman will clarify procedure to the board, identifying the particular issues on which board members will ask questions at least in the early part of the interview. The HoD may be the only mathematician on the board. Alternatively, an adviser or a senior colleague with a mathematics background may modify the breadth of our concerns. The chief purpose of interview questions is to allow the candidates to give of their best and is not to trip them into error! It is usually helpful to start with a non-threatening question that allows the candidate to talk easily to the panel. Follow up questions can be more incisive exploring depth of thinking, experience, commitment etc.

Post interview discussion will review the record and the impression created by each of the candidates and hopefully a unanimous decision will be reached. We may feel more or less influential in this debate, the latter may well be the case, particularly if the school is looking for contributions outside mathematics. The practice of expecting an immediate decision from a candidate offered the job is of debatable merit and is certainly not practised in many industrial and commercial fields. There is much to be said for a considered response following further reflection and consultation by the candidate who may well suffer from being the isolated decision maker, away from family, professional advisers etc. By comparison, the employer has gathered a group to make this decision.

6) *CLOSE THE PROCEEDINGS*

The stage immediately following the appointment is crucial. The elated successful candidate may perhaps be having a chat with senior colleagues or be taken over by members of the department who have waited after school to see the results. Spare a thought, however, for those who are unsuccessful. They have worked hard, may feel very disappointed and might well benefit from a few words of encouragement. Views on the value of debriefing vary greatly but recognising the particular strengths of candidates can help them in the next interview; warning of special weaknesses may be done with good intention but could get us unnecessarily into deep water!

The newly appointed colleague will appreciate an invitation to visit the department for a day when the timetable and classes can be discussed in detail. In some senses membership of the mathematics team operates from the moment that the candidate shakes the Head's hand in accepting the post.

Professional development

Training and experience are both essential if a teacher is to be able to develop properly. Depending upon the locality, in-service training is often available locally at teacher centres, education colleges and university departments of education. The DES organises courses on a regional and national basis. The mathematics teachers' associations, in addition to local branch activities, and their annual conferences, arrange courses and conferences on an ad hoc basis in response to current areas of interest. In recent years, the MA diploma and the specialist dipolmas for teachers of low attainers and for heads of department have been major growth areas with many colleges offering approved courses. In recent years, many members of the profession and in particular local authorities have put a greater emphasis on school-based activity, encouraging schemes for self assessment and development. The appointment of advisory teachers has enabled such activity to develop in a variety of interesting ways. The introduction of (GRIST) funding for in-service work in 1987 has produced new opportunities but also considerable uncertainty about the future form of training. In particular the viability of relatively expensive long courses is in doubt.

It seems worth developing a departmental plan for in-service training which is likely to be implemented over a number of years rather than within any one year. The plan might usefully be divided into two parts (a) in-house and (b) externally provided. It is desirable that all members of the department should feel involved in such a programme and it may exercise many of our diplomatic talents to ensure that the reluctant participate and the inveterate course-goers don't exclude the shy, modest and professionally inert members of the department. In-house activity might be intended for an individual or a small group, e.g. develop Peter Smith's skills in working with low attainers, enable Jane Trump to use a microcomputer in her classroom work, develop skills in using the new SMP 11–16 individualised materials with the first year teachers. Alongside such a programme there will be a plan for activities for the whole department. They might involve the use of departmental meetings and of LEA-provided in-service days. Activities will ideally draw on the talent and experience which exist in the department.

Possible activities:

- Short introductory talks by members of the department about the way they tackle a topic, followed by discussion.
- Contributing ideas on day to day work in the classroom e.g. 'kinds of homework', 'good fillers for the last ten minutes of a lesson', 'using a poster to start a discussion'.
- Session run by an advisory teacher or college tutor.
- Discussion of a current issue or of a previously circulated article.
- Viewing a video of some mathematics teaching interspersed with discussion.
- Use of SMP In-Service Resource Kits or the Shell Centre boxes relating to problem solving etc.

The HoD's role is seen to be one of identifying the need and facilitating the activity but where possible avoiding the danger of providing most of the input! Recognition of this danger may be a relief to the HoD *and* to the department.

In relation to external provision a number of differing course types can be identified:

Professional organisation conferences, courses, meetings (evening, day, week), e.g. MA/ATM Conference.

Specific issues (brief course/meeting) information provision and discussion of implications, e.g. GCSE for maths, research report, curriculum project, HoD briefing.

Specific development of teaching skills (one week intensive or series of regular meetings), e.g. micros in mathematics teaching, teaching A-level mathematics, maths for low attainers, OU, in-service package.

General updating in relation to subject teaching (full time secondment or substantial part-time programme), an opportunity to reassess aims and means in teaching mathematics, e.g. recent developments in mathematics teaching, associateship or study attachment.

Training for head of department role (full time or year long part-time programme), e.g. post-Cockcroft courses offered, specialist MA, diploma course.

Further applied academic course (one year full time/two years part-time), e.g. M.Ed., M.Sc.(Ed.) with varying amounts of 'mathematics' and other educational issues alongside mathematics education.

Research programmes leading to an award, e.g. Advanced Diploma, M.Phil., Ph.D.

Suggestions for action

i) *In-service opportunities should contribute to the work of the department as well as the individuals. (Implications – mutual support, interest and opportunity for feedback.)*

ii) *Involvement in courses which may be initiated by teacher or HoD; consultation over purpose and practicalities to be normal practice.*

iii) *An annual review of experience and outline planning of future activity to be carried out with external activity related to internal in-service work.*

iv) *Ensure that information arrives from local and more distant providers and that it is displayed or is accessible to colleagues in the department.*

v) *Encourage particular colleagues to attend specific courses where appropriate in relation to departmental needs and with respect to their own professional development.*

vi) *For each course attended:*
   a) *clarify purpose and departmental interest by pre-course discussions with colleagues*
   b) *keep in touch with developments, demands and scope for feedback*
   c) *require brief, written report for departmental file*
   d) *hold de-briefing to ascertain*
      - *appropriate content and form of feedback*
      - *informal evaluation of course.*

vii) *Structure feedback session to ensure it is worthwhile. Avoid lengthy summaries of a year's work! Work on some specific issues or activities which make an impact.*

viii) *Keep in touch with LEA adviser:*
   a) *requesting courses/activities not available*
   b) *informing about in-service strategy and progress*
   c) *providing feedback on courses attended by colleagues.*

ix) *Where possible, talk with HMIs, teachers' centre wardens, tutors in training institutions about course experiences and provision needed.*

Career progression

Career progression in the teaching profession as in any other, owes much to the random factors of opportunity, place and time. For some whose path is smooth, rapid promotion 'proves' their skill, determination and superiority, whilst for others on a harder track, 'bad luck' and an 'unappreciative Headmaster' constantly dog their footsteps, thwarting ambition and causing despair. Over recent years changes to the salary structure have gradually reduced the number of scales to which a teacher can be promoted and demographic factors have also reduced the opportunities for promotion. National measures will be required to materially alleviate the position.

Much of our previous discussion relates to the need to demonstrate that we value the work of the teachers in our department. We shall consider the following activities in which we are engaged:

Staff appraisal
Internal promotion
Promotion beyond the school
Teachers experiencing major problems.

1) *STAFF APPRAISAL*

External pressure to introduce formal procedures for staff appraisal caused considerable dissent in the mid eighties when the proposals were linked to decisions about salaries. The concept of appraisal itself, when attached to schemes for further training, has not been so contentious. Informal appraisal takes place all the time, influencing many decisions that we take almost on a daily basis - the allocation of teaching groups, who is to be given the task of introducing a new scheme, who will set an internal exam paper, are all examples of this, separate from the career decisions of who is to gain promotion. Much appraisal takes place at a subconscious level so that changing to a formal process requires the acquisition of new skills. The main difference, and the chief advantage, is that the formal process involves discussion with the member of staff concerned. In some schools the formality is taken to the point of producing written, agreed reports of the discussion.

A good teacher is often acutely aware of personal difficulties and failings and in an atmosphere of mutual trust will value positive advice. Problems usually need putting into perspective before they can be satisfactorily resolved. Recognising aspects worthy of praise and ensuring that these form part of the discussion are as important as points of criticism.

None of this can take place unless a great deal of preparation has been done. It helps if a date and time for the discussion can be agreed in advance and if other matters are then not allowed to intrude. The teacher may well have particular ideas to introduce and a positive atmosphere can be encouraged if the broad areas for discussion are agreed in advance. At the meeting an appropriate balance between the overly formal and the casual has to be struck if the outcome is to be constructive. Our colleagues will doubtless be happy to receive praise and encouragement for their current work and future prospects. There is much greater scope for dissent when the appraisal involves the identification of negative aspects of performance and of appropriate action. Most of us may prefer to steer well clear of such dangerous ground but this will invalidate the whole process. Particular care must be exercised in commenting on aspects of a colleague's personality which appear to cause difficulties. Such comments can be very threatening to most of us. In this matter and other less sensitive ones, we shall need to identify constructive ways forward with the provision of appropriate support. Clearly our colleagues' self-identified 'weaknesses' offer the most promising starting point. There is little doubt that this is an area in which we must be modest and be prepared to learn through consultation, training and experience. (Ted Wragg's practical guide *Teacher Appraisal* (Macmillan, 1987) may be found helpful.)

2) *INTERNAL PROMOTION*

When a colleague has worked hard, given more to the department and school than others, taken advantage of opportunities to increase and extend skills, then promotion is naturally deserved.

The implications of the promoted posts scheme are still being worked out and it appears that it may be several years before the position stabilises. We shall usually have to make a case which will withstand the competing claims of colleagues from other departments. The shortage of mathematics teachers usually makes this a somewhat easier task. Indeed the designer of the new scheme had the retention of teachers in particular disciplines in mind when proposing the change.

Appointment to a promoted post will normally carry specific extra responsibilities. There is little difficulty in making a list of tasks and duties suitable for delegation, which could materially improve the work of the department. Nevertheless, promotion can come to a member of our department for undertaking responsibilities outside the department. It can be particularly galling to lose the full time services of a colleague whose work is particularly valued. Nevertheless, it is an unhealthy school that is totally departmentalised and the school, department and teacher can all ultimately benefit from a broadening of interest.

3) *PROMOTION BEYOND THE SCHOOL*

When teachers seek promotion to another school, either because the internal promotion path is blocked or for other reasons, we are likely to have a part to play in preparing the reference which has been requested from our Headteacher. Usually at short notice, we may be asked either to provide a written report or to meet the Head to discuss what should go into the reference. With the high demand for promoted posts, our report may be very influential in getting our colleague to the interview. A tension between personal and professional loyalties may inevitably exist at times.

Usually a job description is sent which allows us to make specific comments and occasionally a form is enclosed asking precise questions. However it is still quite common to receive requests which are very vague in relation to what the inquirer wants to know. Nevertheless a reference which fails to cover an expected area, risks misinterpretation by a Head who is adept at 'reading between the lines'.

In the absence of specific requests, the general areas to be covered may be listed as follows:

i) Health (frequency of absences), punctuality
ii) Reliability and commitment
iii) Personality and relationships with pupils/colleagues
iv) Classroom manner and discipline
v) Extra-departmental and extra-curricular involvement
vi) Likely performance at interview

Few of us would wish to stress weaknesses but a failure to mention any may weaken the credibility of the reference or undermine the colleagues' chances at interview. It is not easy to live up to unrealistic expectations!

If the appointment is being made at a local school we may be contacted directly by our opposite number at the school for an oral report. Some might regard this as improper but others would consider that the resulting communication will be more useful than the formally written reference. In giving any 'off-the-cuff' oral report we do run the risk of giving a partial account where only certain elements are picked up by the hearer and transferred to those responsible for the appointment. Professional judgement has to be exercised, often at short notice!

Some colleagues may need to be encouraged to seek wider experiences through promotion in a different school. The known environment can be attractive, but too long in one school can be stunting and may ultimately prove to be an obstacle to promotion. Finally, we need to recognise that some of our current colleagues will be HoDs themselves in future (what sort of model are we presenting to them?). Some of them may become headteachers, advisers, teacher trainers, inspectors. Is our thinking and planning about promotion sufficiently broad to respond to this?

4) *TEACHERS EXPERIENCING MAJOR PROBLEMS*

All teachers have problems and weaknesses which become manifest with particular pupils in particular situations. However the weak teacher seems able to manufacture a difficult situation where none at first exists! It can provide problems which will daunt the most confident and experienced of us! Inexperience is the greatest weakness in a teacher and explains why we need to give so much thought and support to probationary teachers. It is usually a temporary condition that slowly but surely improves. We should not be immediately despondent, even if an experienced teacher goes through a difficult patch. It is disconcerting to have to provide extra support for no apparent reason and it certainly tests our confidence in a teacher when current performance belies our expectations. Inevitably we question our own judgement at such a time and perhaps confidence is only fully restored when the problems are finally resolved.

A competent teacher weakened by sickness or emotional stress can go through a terrible period of disciplinary problems, the problems often beginning before anyone is aware of the cause. Those who are physically ill will usually see a doctor and refrain from work until restored to good health, the disciplinary problems abating as quickly as they arose. Emotional stress can however cause seemingly inexplicable changes of personality which in severe cases may develop into a crisis leading to breakdown before medical help is sought. It certainly emphasises the need to be aware and sensitive to colleagues' problems.

At some stage we may find ourselves having to deal with a 'failing' teacher. Such a person is evidently very ineffective in the classroom as a teacher and there are almost certainly major related discipline problems. The person appears not to be responding to support and advice and may even fail to recognise the inadequacy of their work. In teaching, it is difficult in practice to provide a sheltered working environment for someone with such major problems. We should not feel reluctant to share such a problem with senior colleagues. It can be very helpful to keep a written 'diary' of relevant events since later discussions may be clarified by an accurate record of developments.

Appropriate action may depend on the stage in the teacher's career. Are they in their probationary year, have they recently been appointed on the professional scale, after teaching in another school, do they receive a responsibility payment? Whichever the case, the Head is likely to be aware of the situation and if all internal measures have been exhausted, may decide to seek outside help from the advisory service. Counselling from outside the school by an adviser, together with observation in the classroom may lead to a gradual change for the better. A modified timetable may be thought necessary or, more drastically, a change of school. A teacher in such a difficult situation may, given the opportunity to reflect on their position without becoming unduly defensive, decide that it would be better to resign from teaching. Throughout this traumatic period we shall need to exercise considerable tact and diplomacy as we resolve the inevitable difficulties which result from both pupils and other colleagues while exercising some faith in the knowledge that apparently 'hopeless cases' in the past have responded and finally become satisfactory teachers.

In an extreme case the problems that arise in the period leading up to the dismissal of a teacher are acutely distressful. A teacher in such a predicament will probably be very distrustful and may well blame the school for all that has happened. Caught between a colleague, desperately in need of help, and the pupils enduring incompetent teaching is a most uncomfortable situation to be in.

The process of dismissal is painfully slow but is designed to ensure fairness to the teacher. The Head of Department will be under specific instructions in the later stages but will have been advised to adopt formal procedures at an earlier date. It is often agreed to give instructions in writing; the procedure offering a way to avoid misunderstandings and conflict. If this procedure is adopted then copies of all such written instructions and of replies need to be kept for future reference.

At this point it is probably appropriate to raise the relatively rare occurrence where the problems arise from serious misconduct rather than from serious underperformance; for instance, cases of misrepresentation of qualifications, undisclosed dismissal, misuse of schools funds, sexual involvement with pupils. The crisis is likely to develop rapidly and probably unexpectedly. Dealing with it will certainly involve other senior staff and our greatest difficulty may arise from maintaining professional loyalty while dealing with a departmental colleague.

The proceedings leading to dismissal are inevitably disturbing but having accepted the post of Head of Department, we really have no choice but to play our full part. It is after all in no one's best interest, least of all the failed teacher, to allow the situation to persist. The greatest service we can provide for these very few colleagues is to remove them from the classroom. We would do well to remember our fundamental concern for the mathematical education of our pupils when such issues come to the fore.

Conclusion

Management of the department is one of the most challenging aspects of our work as a HoD. Carrying it out may make us feel isolated at times and we may feel this justifies the additional salary received. Yet the most effective managers are usually those who establish a style which engenders a spirit of co-operation, involvement and respect tinged with the knowledge that even middle managers have to take difficult decisions on occasions. A school contains several people exercising a similar management function; neighbouring schools have other heads of mathematics departments. Our professional skills as managers will develop through interaction with them, both informally and through structured in-service activity.

5 Administration

Most professionals have a dislike of the demands of administration, but few welcome a disorganised and chaotic working environment. It seems desirable for administration to play an unobtrusive yet positive role in enabling the department to achieve its goals. The design and implementation of an appropriate system usually falls to us, though the way in which the school administration operates may be expected to have some influence on what happens in the various departments. This chapter will consider a number of issues which seem of particular importance.

Communication

Many of the situations confronting us are common to other departments, and indeed to posts of responsibility in other organisations; hence many of the problems of communication are of a general nature and discussions with others, even outside school life, can sometimes be helpful in understanding the problems and in finding solutions. Problems of communication are not always to do with information not being circulated, but have to do with whether people feel they have been consulted and involved in the decision making processes. In analysing the communication which occurs within the department it is possible to identify:

Decision making and discussion. There are situations where debate between two or more members of the department, and possibly all the department, will help to clarify and crystallise a matter of departmental policy.

Conveying enthusiasm; providing encouragement and support. The feelings and attitudes of the members of the department are extremely important to their functioning, both individually and as a team.

Sharing experiences and ways of teaching. We will often be interested in the approaches being taken to different topics by our colleagues and may wish to discuss or advise.

Providing information

i) *Long term information.* This involves those facts about the functioning of the department which will remain relevant over the course of a school year or longer, but will occasionally require modification or addition; this will probably include teaching schemes, procedures for issuing and collecting textbooks, lost books, a list of available teaching resources and record keeping procedures.

ii) *Medium term information.* Some matters assume vital importance during a limited period and then become redundant; for example, who is setting and marking internal exams, books out of stock.

iii) *Short term information.* Day to day matters, such as covering for absent colleagues or advertising a course or lecture, often call for quick transit of information.

iv) *Background information.* We can help the members of the department keep up to date with new books, magazine articles, reports of working parties etc.

In order to ensure that such communications occur we have various techniques at our disposal:

a) A written (possibly duplicated) note to all (or relevant) members of the department; it may be helpful to state the period of its applicability and whether it is to be added to a departmental 'handbook' (see (b) below).

b) A departmental 'handbook' consisting of relevant long term information, such as to be of particular value to a new member of the department. As additions and modifications of this information will be required a looseleaf format would be desirable. (Appendix 5.1 provides a list of possible section headings.)

c) A note on a maths notice-board in a common room or maths office, if there is one. The efficiency of this depends on how often colleagues are able or willing to peruse such notice-boards.

d) A single document headed with the names of intended readers which circulates around them in turn; this sometimes involves a need to monitor its progress.

e) An individual note to all relevant colleagues asking them to consult a longer document which has been placed in a convenient situation.

f) A full departmental meeting.

g) A meeting of some of the department who are particularly concerned with the matters to be discussed e.g. those who teach a particular year group or course.

h) Informal chats at break etc..
i) More formal or confidential discussion with an individual member of the department.

In deciding which means of communication to adopt for a given need, factors such as the size of the department, school geography, timetable and individual personalities are likely to be relevant. In addition the points below have been found useful by some departments and are offered here for consideration:

i) *Meetings.* Full departmental meetings at regular intervals are found to be of great value in many schools but there may be little value in using such meetings for purposes which could be fulfilled by other means, particularly by a written note. If meetings are to succeed they must be felt to be important by those attending and therefore relevant to their needs. In some schools it is thought desirable and possible to hold departmental meetings within the timetabled day but at others such meetings take place at lunch-time, after school or even at home during the evening; meetings coupled with some social activity have been found to provide useful motivation. The introduction of 'directed time' has often led to clarification of the school's commitment to departmental meetings and of teachers' obligations.

ii) *Minutes.* The minutes of departmental meetings form a useful record of discussions and decisions; they may be circulated to all and possibly added to a central departmental handbook. They may be most useful in a terse, note form but marking explicit decisions taken, dates for action etc.

iii) *Informality.* If conversation flags at break, a brief account of an interesting classroom situation or piece of mathematics can spark off a useful discussion but care needs to be exercised that one does not become a bore or create a 'clique' of the department; reading between the lines of colleagues' responses may be vital! The tone of a written or spoken comment can significantly affect its reception. Phrases such as 'would it be possible . . .', 'should we consider . . .' and 'please' have their value.

iv) *Controversy.* When tackling a controversial issue where it is known that there may be strong differing feelings in the department, initial individual discussions with colleagues can help to determine the approach to be taken in the subsequent discussion at a full meeting.

v) *Personal conversation.* Some situations can be sufficiently personal to a particular member of the department that a confidential discussion is required. It can be remarkably difficult to find a time and place within a school to permit such an arrangement without fear of interruption from staff or pupils. However, difficult situations can drift on if they are not suitably dealt with, and we must sometimes 'grasp the nettle'. Informal discussion can be useful but if any particular decision has been made, it can easily be forgotten or misinterpreted if it is not subsequently confirmed on paper.

vi) *Delegation.* Not all communication within the department need directly involve the HoD; we may be able to delegate and encourage various forms of interaction between the members of the department; this could include the writing of minutes of meetings.

It often seems difficult for those in positions of responsibility to receive useful feedback on the efficiency of their own functioning and we may need to consider how best to monitor the effectiveness of the communication within the department. We can develop a sensitivity to:

a) obvious, and often public, blunders; there can be a temptation to cast blame on everyone or anyone else, but constructive self-criticism may be more beneficial.
b) asking individuals or groups for their view of the success of a particular matter, making it known that constructive criticism would be welcomed.
c) members of the department who take the initiative in approaching us with positive comments.
d) members of the department who make 'veiled' comments, from which we may glean useful information if we can interpret them or encourage more explicit discussion.

Finance

Initially, we may find the control of funds a novel or a daunting experience. It may be the first time we have had the chance to spend somebody else's money! The administrative procedures involved vary between schools and areas. First, there is a need to understand the system of allocating funds to the department. How does your Head operate? In some cases the Head will distribute money between departments by his own traditional formula, others will request planned budgets from us and in some cases there may be more democratic procedures involving discussions with Deputy Heads and HoDs. Some Heads will publish the figures for each department, others keep them confidential. Some Heads are unperturbed by over expenditure (although it will probably be taken back in the subsequent year) whereas others are sufficiently concerned about this possibility that they tend to underspend.

We also need to know whether the funds allocated to the department have to be spent by a certain date and whether the Head witholds some reserves for allocation later in the year when there may be specific requests for further finance. In general, however, the bulk of the department's income will come from the annual sum allocated by the Head. If we feel that our department is being poorly funded (and most do!) attempts to seek a substantial increase should perhaps be preceded by questions such as 'Are my requests realistic and backed up by sound reasoning?', 'Can I prove that money I have spent in the past has been profitably and efficiently used?'

A change in curriculum, requiring different books and materials or the acquisition of major teaching resources, will certainly require substantial money and the educational justification for such developments needs to be clearly stated, possibly with evidence from other schools which have already implemented such changes. Local authority advisers can often support such projects, perhaps verbally and sometimes with direct financial assistance. Sometimes the cost of a large item may be spread over more than one financial year. There can be benefit in planning and asking for a budget for a period of two to five years ahead.

During the year, specific needs may arise and the Head will need to be approached with a view to releasing unallocated funds. Another source of income in some schools is from Parents' Associations or School Trust Funds. Those responsible for them are often anxious to see a specific item purchased on their behalf, computers being a common example in recent years. Occasionally a specific project may qualify for a grant from an external trust, business etc.

Having understood the school system and the potential sources of funding, how are decisions about expenditure to be reached at departmental level? Will there be discussions involving members of the department with an openness about procedures and ultimate decision making? While we will carry the final responsibility, colleagues may have good ideas to contribute and strong feelings about open participation. A framework to respond to this needs to be carefully thought through if frustration on their part is to be avoided and if we are still to be able to use funds for purposeful development.

In seeking to obtain maximum value from the money which is available, we may ask 'What will be of most benefit to pupils and staff?' We may find, for example, that some teachers and pupils make no use of the explanations and examples in textbooks. It may then be advisable to buy other resource materials such as a supply of models, extension and interest materials or even suitable sets of graded exercises which are often cheaper. Gradually the department may develop a substantial library of such resources. There may be situations when providing teachers with reference books proves more productive than providing each of their pupils with another textbook.

When considering a major change in textbooks or teaching schemes which may well involve a commitment to a considerable expense, careful research is necessary to avoid the risk of disappointment. The LEA adviser and staff of other schools can be helpful; inspection copies can be obtained from publishers or teachers' centres. The views of members of the department can be sought; each may, for example, undertake to assess one topic area and its development through the course. Finally it may be possible to experiment with one set of the materials before placing a large order for the whole school.

We will also find ourselves ordering mathematical stationery and teaching aids. In many areas there is a local authority supplier from whom such items are available relatively cheaply; they may also provide a comprehensive catalogue which forms a useful basis for constructing an order. If the local catalogue is of poor quality we might benefit others by suggesting to the suppliers ways in which it could be improved.

The procedure adopted by the school or authority for ordering goods must also be understood; this will usually involve an official school order form and/or providing the necessary documentation for office staff. It is unfortunate to create administrative chaos with one's first order but even worse to establish a reputation for causing havoc in this field.

The management of books and resources

The department is likely to own a very large number of textbooks, some of which may well have been gathering dust for years! Any which are literally falling apart can be thrown out immediately as they can waste or spoil storage space; others may have a little life left in them and can sometimes be useful for the occasion demanding a few more exercises or perhaps the individual gifted pupil looking for some material outside the current standard school course. Sometimes useful pages from old books can be extracted and mounted as work cards.

For the standard course materials, we will need to devise a system by which it is known which classes have possession, and also the condition of these items so that the need to order further copies can be anticipated – delivery time can be several weeks even when no complications arise. A slight surplus of standard texts needs to be carried to allow for lost books and newcomers to the school. (A procedure for considering a new textbook is given in Appendix 5.2.)

When a course of several volumes of textbooks is being followed, it is not always convenient for the change from one volume to the next to occur at the end of the year, or even the end of a term. Unless the department is overstocked this will call for considerable cooperation of timing between members of the staff so that the exchange can occur smoothly, preventing some sets being left without a book or having to relinquish a book before it has completed its purpose, although that is not to say that mathematics can never be taught without access to book or printed material! If possible, it is often worth holding an excess of at least one set of such materials so that there is room for some flexibility in timing – even then we will need to ensure that there is adequate communication between staff.

As well as textbooks retained by pupils, many departments keep a single set of some books (particularly question books) which are issued to a group just for a single period or possibly for a few days. There may also be other such resources (e.g. SMP, SMILE materials). Some form of booking system is then needed so that staff can be sure that the books will be available when they want them. For these books especially, a central store is essential. Separate containers are often useful and if commercial ones are too expensive, strong well-labelled cardboard boxes often suffice. Such a system gives immediate indication of which materials staff are finding useful so that further copies of popular items can be purchased.

Having spent considerable sums on teaching materials, it is essential to ensure that they last as long as possible. Most books, especially those with a soft cover benefit from reinforcement of edges and spines with tape (masking tape often seems more effective than transparent tape) and a cover of heavy paper. It is then very helpful to mark the cover clearly with the name of the book. Pupils need to be encouraged to keep books in good condition; some schools grade the condition of each book on issue but if this is thought to be unrealistic, it is helpful to ensure that all the books issued to a particular set are in similar condition so that any subsequent misuse becomes more obvious. Some departments give each book an individual number and keep a record of which book has been issued to which pupil. When loss or damage does occur there is a need for a consistent policy, which may well be a school-based one, for action to be taken. This will often involve reimbursement (where legal) from the pupil and we may feel it appropriate that all such negotiations are with ourselves rather than involving other members of the department. The individual teacher may be able to reduce the wear and tear on books by informing pupils in advance which books should be brought to a particular lesson.

To make the fullest use of the variety of stock which may be held, each teacher needs to be familiar with the materials available and to have easy access to them. A staff departmental library can be a great asset in this respect since it can include one copy of each such item, in addition to a wide variety of other reference books, journals, articles etc.; a file of ideas used by individual teachers can also be maintained.

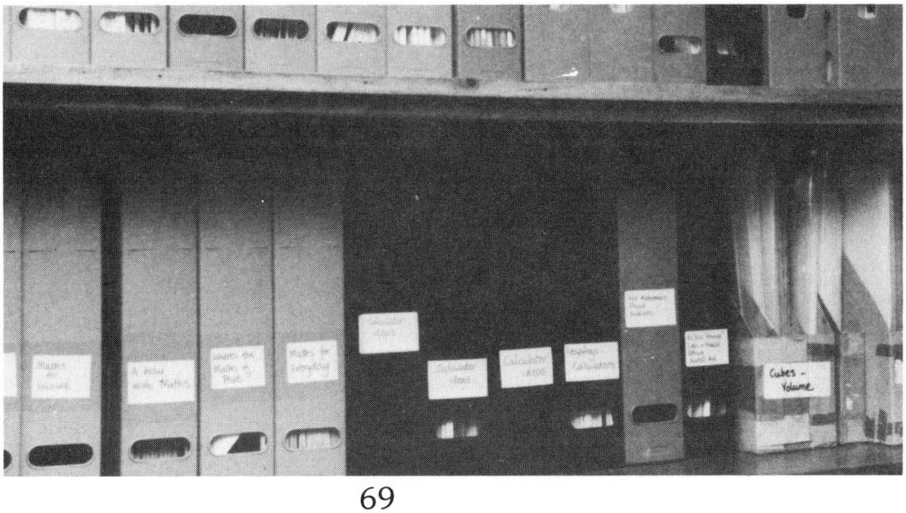

The material resources of the department will usually include such items as grid papers, models, OHP transparencies, video tapes and publishers' and suppliers' catalogues. It is useful for each teacher to have a list of these and easy access to them. Again, it is useful to monitor the amount of stock held and to reorder in good time; this is a task which some have delegated and have found that this has the advantage of familiarising colleagues with the resources at first hand!

In addition to resources within the school, there are often others which can be borrowed from elsewhere. Staff can also be provided with such details as the availability of films etc., contents of the local teachers' centre, speakers from universities etc.

Allocation of staff to teaching groups

The procedure for writing the timetable differs from school to school but we are usually involved at some stage in determining how staff will be deployed during the following year; we may not have a completely free choice because of other timetable constraints and will then have to exercise our judgement on priorities.

Power at last - a chance to dictate other people's future! Do we sit down to this task with a sense of dictatorial delight or of neurotic nervousness, afraid of upsetting someone - or everyone? How can we go about this crucial task in a reasonable way? Some particular issues are identified in what follows:

Initial discussions with the Head and, in the case of shared staff, with other HoDs, to decide the manpower needs and resources of the department. If possible, potential numbers of pupils and staff changes are useful items of information as early as possible.

Continuity. To what extent do we wish staff to stay with the same teaching group for another year, in 6th form, in 4th/5th forms and in lower years? This will determine some fixed points to the structure.

Needs of a particular teaching group. Has a particular form/set shown a special need e.g. by containing some exceptional pupils at either end of the ability range, or special discipline problems? Can they be given a member of staff who will be able to answer these needs?

Staff strengths and weaknesses. Have these been identified? Should staff stick to their familiar areas or be encouraged to others? – this needs to be answered for each individual. Is there a danger of a teacher getting 'into a rut' or do some function very effectively and usefully from their rut?

Consultation. Are members of the department to be consulted at any stage about their 'lot' for next year? If so, what form will this take? There may be conflicts, how will these be resolved? Can this be used as an opportunity for down to earth discussion between the HoD and his colleagues?

Sharing of sets between staff. In the 6th form this is often desirable or essential to make use of individual expertise: is it desirable lower down the school? The Cockcroft Report suggests not, but not all would agree with this view. We must find an arrangement which maximises the motivation and learning of pupils without putting intolerable burdens on staff.

Draft schemes can now be attempted, columns with names of staff across the top are found to be useful by many, sets can be listed down the left hand side, certainties can be penned in and possibilities pencilled in.

Left overs may appear at the end of the scheme, i.e. some staff with a small number of periods unfilled from their appropriate quota. These can be allocated to specific projects such as small remedial groups, administrative tasks, curriculum development etc. It is important that the distribution of work is seen to be fair!

In addition to the allocation of teaching groups the delegation of departmental responsibilities can add both to the experience of colleagues and to the smooth running of the department (Appendix 5.3 gives a listing of responsibilities in a particular school).

Internal assessment

The concept of assessment has become very much broader in recent years; written examinations were once considered as the heart of assessment but now there is increasing emphasis on pupils' skills in oral, practical and investigatory mathematics; these factors have been considered in Chapter 2, but here we must note that they impose considerable administrative requirements.

There is a need to define the purposes of internal assessment and to consider the subsequent use of the data, since this may indicate how the system is to be organised.

Materials must be collected or written, tested and frequently examined for their effectiveness; this will probably include such items as:

- Guidelines and pro formas for classroom assessment of oral questions and comments from pupils, written work, practical work, willingness and ability in carrying out investigations
- Bank of investigations and problem situations – with some categorising in terms of their appropriateness for different ages and abilities
- Bank of practical tasks and easy access to the necessary equipment
- Supply of suitably graded mental arithmetic materials
- GCSE coursework items.

In most schools the full implementation of such schemes is in its infancy and the administration of these tasks is still being developed; we must ensure that members of our department are fully involved in planning and execution and that their role is made as easy as possible by good communication and convenient access to all the appropriate materials at the required time. In an area of curriculum exploration and development, such as this, communication between schools can also be of enormous value.

In addition to such forms of continuous assessment many schools maintain a system of end of year and/or mid-year examinations arranged on a school basis; the objectives may include:

i) Giving an incentive to pupils to work and revise
ii) Providing pupils and staff with an objective assessment of individual attainment and progress
iii) Monitoring the general progress of a teaching group and the effectiveness of the teaching it has received; this may involve the appropriateness and value of items in the curriculum of the group
iv) Comparing the ability of a group with previous years
v) Assessing the effectiveness of test items.

To enable us to draw any such conclusions from the final data requires considerable planning and forethought. We may need a particular period of time for each exam, possibly with several groups of pupils taking the same paper concurrently; such details need to be clarified with the colleague responsible for the administration of the school exams.

The writing of exam papers is likely to be a task which is shared with other members of the department who will need to know the precise syllabus content and whether they should consult other staff involved in the teaching of the group concerned; where two papers are being set the aims of each will need to be distinguished and agreed. A realistic and efficient mark scheme will also be necessary.

Where the papers are written to include spaces for working and answers the marking is usually easier and by arranging separate sections to include questions on particular topic areas, marks may be distinguished and a profile of pupil performance constructed. If some test items are retained, possibly with minor modifications, from year to year, a comparison of different year groups becomes more reliable.

In analysing and interpreting the results we must be aware of the danger of jumping to apparently obvious conclusions – if a set does badly, it may be of lower ability than we thought, rather than any inadequacy in the teaching involved. The results can be displayed in columns so that the performance of different sets can be compared; this can indicate the accuracy (some would say the value) of setting. Analysing the marks by individual questions or groups of questions can suggest problems or successes which have arisen in the teaching and can then influence decisions over the teaching approach or content in the following year. It is also useful for the setter or marker to write some brief notes on the effectiveness of the exam and individual test items in it, which can be referred to when considering the following year's exam. This is one of the many areas where we can learn from experience and act upon it. (Further details on procedures relating to internal examinations are given in Appendix 5.4.)

External examinations

In most schools one (or two) of the department have responsibility for external examination entries and administration. We can ensure that the correct code numbers and options are known to this colleague; he may also check that the appropriate tables, formulae booklets and sheets are in the possession of the administrator and that pupils are aware of the contents of such aids, the expected rubric of each paper and whether calculators are permitted. With many candidates taking a variety of different exams, this can be confusing and it is often helpful to provide the information in writing to all those involved.

It is often stated that exam results should not be the only factor in considering a school's (or a department's) functioning; this implies however that it is one important means of monitoring the success of classroom teaching. Any direct comparison between schools is difficult because of their different catchment areas, entrance policies etc. However such exercises need not be totally meaningless, particularly if individual subjects are separately analysed.

We can examine our department's results in a number of ways, including the following:

i) Calculate the average grade for a particular exam and compare it with similar figures for recent years – this may disclose a trend.
ii) Compare grades of individual pupils with their performances in internal exams and their teacher's predicted grade.
iii) Compare the maths grade of each individual pupil with the average grade obtained in external exams of all other subjects taken by the same pupil at the same time; it should be noted that there are national variations between pass rates of different subjects (e.g. a consistently higher proportion of candidates have achieved grades A, B and C at English O-level than in Mathematics).

It can also be helpful to keep a record of the GCSE level achievement of A-level candidates, since this experience can be used when advising pupils on the wisdom of starting an A-level course.

Particular groups of pupils with poor results should be identified and explanations found; it may be that too much was expected from them, and this may indicate that a different examination policy should be considered for similar groups in the future.

Staff records

For most of us, memory is usually stretched to its limit and keeping a systematic written record of relevant staff details can relieve this pressure. This information can be useful in writing references for promotion or redeployment in addition to enabling us to assess the effective and fair use of colleagues' time and talents, filling gaps in experience etc. Some schools operate a system of formal appraisal of staff on an annual basis.

Useful information can include:

i) Academic qualifications and initial training for teaching
ii) Courses attended
iii) Previous teaching experience
iv) Experience gained in present post, sets taught
v) Delegated tasks
vi) Notable successes
vii) Extra-departmental interests/responsibilities

Such information needs to be stored with care but with the increasing tendency towards access to personal information, it seems inappropriate to store information other than fairly straightforward factual data relating to the job done.

Pupil records

There will usually be a well defined system for keeping pupil records at a central school level; in some cases this may include subject details such as progress in mathematics. However many departments find it useful to keep their own information for situations such as:

i) Pupils changing teacher
ii) Pupils leaving to join a new school
iii) Parental enquiry to HoD or teacher
iv) Pupils seeking acceptance to an advanced course
v) Pupils who have left school or are unavailable and a report of other information is required.

Keeping such information up to date can be a time-consuming task and only those items which are felt to be really useful need be stored; they may include:

i) Assessment data throughout school career
ii) External exam results
iii) Copy of reports sent to parents
iv) Tutor group; maths set and teachers
v) Feeder school information
vi) Further education and career ambitions
vii) Comments received from parents.

Bumph, filing and memory

For most of us, hardly a day goes by without some letter, circular, catalogue etc. being passed in our direction. Together with other documents, such as past exam papers, higher education details and records, systematic storage (and disposal!) is a significant part of our task.

There seems little substitute for a clearly labelled filing system, using some or all of the following: filing cabinet, box files, lever arch files, ring files, manilla folders. It can sometimes seem self-indulgent to be spending money on such administrative items where there is probably a shortage of funds for text-books, but the department can only function well when we feel confident and in reasonable control of our surroundings and other members of the department have good access to relevant documentation. Furthermore we need to have a convenient location for this storage and may feel justified in making a case to the Head if it is not presently available.

Filing will often be by subjects but some have based part of their system on time, so that documents can be found by knowing when they were produced or which time of the year they become relevant. Many also find it helpful to keep a diary of administrative tasks and necessary documentation throughout the year so that it can be consulted and events anticipated during the following year.

Teaching rooms

The arrangement for allocation of staff to rooms varies from school to school, but it is our responsibility to ensure that teaching staff are able to work effectively and have good access to all available materials. In most cases the preference is for each individual to teach all or most periods in the same room, provided this does not condemn some staff to the continuous use of very poor rooms.

We can ensure that each room used for mathematics has adequate blackboard, display space, furniture and lighting as well as a supply of the commonly-used materials such as grid papers. Ideally it would be equipped with other aids such as blackboard geometrical instruments and an overhead projector with screen, facilities for the easy use of video equipment and a microcomputer are vital. Hopefully rooms will have posters and other display materials which can often be rotated around to different rooms to give a variety of stimulation for pupils.

With increasing emphasis on practical work it may be difficult to provide every room with all the required equipment; if rooms have to be widely spread over the school, a central store is not always convenient either. It may then be necessary to equip one or two rooms as specialist 'laboratories' and for staff to exchange rooms by some agreed scheme.

Posters can often cover some peeling walls but we need also to comment on the general state of decor in the teaching rooms and to do everything possible to ensure that this is of a standard compatible with good teaching and learning. The creation of a 'mathematical environment' is a challenge which many schools have only recently begun to consider.

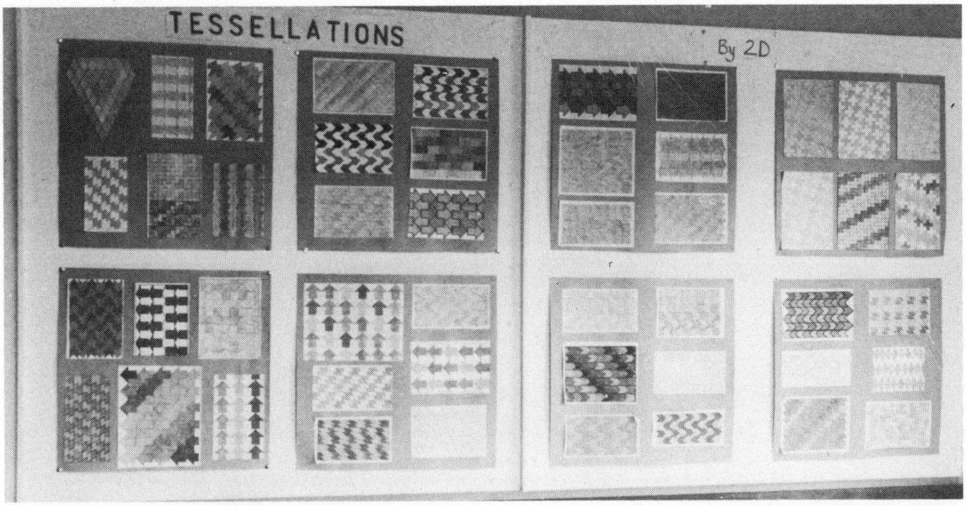
TESSELLATIONS
By 2D

1D AT SIMONSBATH

PROBLEM
PYRAMID
PYRAMID PUZZ
Uses Pythagoras Theorem

General working conditions for staff

Staff common rooms are normally places in which to relax, to enjoy refreshments and to meet colleagues socially and for brief consultations, and for communication of school wide matters through announcements, notice-boards and meetings. Their appearance varies enormously, from uncared for areas of apparent chaos to well designed and maintained facilities for supporting staff in their work. A common-room committee may take responsibility for this part of the school, but our role is important in relation to the working environment provided for members of the department when they are not actually teaching. Many schools have a work room distinct from the common room, but this may be no more than a set of communal tables on which to work.

What are reasonable expectations? In order to prepare lessons, mark books and write materials and reports and to build up a collection of personal teaching resources, a teacher should ideally have his or her own workbase – desk or table, with drawers and cupboard and shelves for textbooks and pupils' exercise books. This may seem dream-like in the face of conditions in some schools, but an awareness of what is desirable can lead to improved conditions. Falling school rolls have sometimes allowed teachers to have their own classrooms as workbases. While not encouraging consultation with colleagues, this has certainly provided the facilities of space and quietness and has enabled individual support to be given to pupils. Less common, but bordering on the ideal, is the becoming available of a whole classroom as a departmental open-plan office, providing work bases for all the teachers and a meeting point for departmental consultations. Achieving such a goal will be largely dependent on our awareness, energy and persuasiveness but it may be instrumental in achieving much of the good practice discussed in this chapter.

Casio-Calculators for education

dairymate

6 Beyond the department

It becomes apparent very quickly that an important part of our role relates to contact with senior management personnel and other professionals outside the department. In some of these contacts we are representing or negotiating on behalf of the department, in others we are seeking support and/or advice from senior colleagues. Establishing appropriate means for communication seems to be an important aim in the first year or two after appointment. Although some of these links may best be maintained by other members of the department, it is often up to us as head of department to take the initiative in establishing them. We shall consider the following:

The hierarchy within the education system
Other departments
Other services within the school
Other schools
Parents
Employers
Training institutions
Examination boards
Teachers' centres
Professional associations

The hierarchy within the educational system

Senior members of the hierarchy may at first be regarded as a threat, particularly where it is clear that we are accountable to some particular post-holder. In practice,such senior colleagues may welcome the style of a head of department who confers and consults with them in respect of departmental aims, achievements and problems. Inevitably the scope for productive consultation will also be dependent on how the other person perceives their role. It may be useful to identify some specific issues and opportunities relating to particular people:

1) *THE HEAD TEACHER*

Some heads have developed, through training or through perception, a management style which relies heavily on consultation with senior staff. They expect to be kept informed of departmental plans and activities – perhaps by means of minutes of departmental meetings, by annual reports and by extended interviews reviewing progress and aspirations. In such a situation we may have a clearer understanding of the Head's thinking which is potentially useful in establishing a strategy for gaining both theoretical and resource support. Even if such positive benefits are not forthcoming, the formal communication in such a situation should make communications necessitated by events easier to handle. But in many schools, the Head's expectations may be less explicit and we may well be uncertain whether consultation will be regarded as a virtue or a sign of weakness. While it is impossible to generalise about such situations where particular personalities and historical precedents may have a major effect, it does seem worth exploring some particular issues to see what kind of professional dialogue can be achieved. Heads can be isolated people who may welcome the opportunity to share, advise and learn.

A good working relationship with the Head may be particularly important in relation to a number of commonly occurring tasks and activities. Table 6.1 lists some activities, together with questions, which may suggest the nature of the working relationship which exists.

The Head Teacher can be a vital catalyst for departmental development. While we may have little, if any, say in the appointment of the Head, our

	Activity	**Possible Indicators**
a)	Appointing a new member of staff	What part is the Head of Department allowed to play in such appointments? • drafting job description • shortlisting • interviewing • making the decision
b)	Dealing with individual staff problems – failing probationer, inadequate or otherwise problem teacher	Is the Head of Department part of a consultative process which determines appropriate action?
c)	Pupils' and parental complaints	Is the Head's professional solidarity a front or a genuine expression of support for a respected colleague in a known situation?
d)	Annual and occasional resource allocation	Is the Head of Department's bid for appropriate funding seriously considered because of its presentation, including supporting evidence?
e)	Curriculum development	Does the Head provide a critical but supportive professional stance in regard to this?
f)	Departmental performance in external examinations	At what kind of level are results discussed – simplistic/defensive/evidence used by the public/starting point for review and possible management decision/educational opportunity?
g)	Staff promotion both within and beyond the school	How is the Head of Department's knowledge of a staff member as a person and as a teacher used in considering promotion or in preparing a reference?

TABLE 6.1

shrewdness and skills in maximising support from this quarter will be a major contribution to the department's work and our teaching colleagues' well-being.

2) *THE SENIOR MANAGEMENT TEAM (SMT)*

As 'management' has achieved a higher profile in schools, so senior management teams have emerged, cabinet-like, to advise the Head and deputies in relation to policy and to implementation. As a head of faculty, a head of maths may be an *ex-officio* member of such a team. More commonly, we may be invited to attend meetings of the SMT only occasionally but may well need to lobby its members from time to time concerning issues such as:

i) resource allocation
ii) professional development for members of the department (perhaps through a professional tutor)
iii) curriculum balance and timetabling (perhaps through a deputy head responsible for curriculum)
iv) room allocation
v) policy issues – homework, reporting on pupil progress, parents' evenings etc.

3) *THE GOVERNORS*

A study of governing bodies which was carried out in the early eighties showed that they perceive their role, and consequently operate, in very different ways. It has become quite common for the head of a major department like mathematics, to be asked to talk about the work of the department to the governors. At the time this is likely to be seen as a ritual or an ordeal, but it should provide us with an opportunity to create more understanding of what mathematics teaching is about and to elicit support perhaps in resource terms and sometimes in relation to experienced and relevantly connected governors. Governing boards usually want to be active, so it is appropriate for us to point the way rather than to be put on the defensive by governors' uninformed initiatives!

4) *LEA ADVISERS/INSPECTORS*

The title used in a particular authority may be indicative of a style or function but it is likely that their job specification is much the same with either label. They are responsible to the Chief Education Officer for the teaching of mathematics in the authority's schools – a mammoth task both in respect of the number of schools and of the limited powers which they hold in relation to the curriculum. In the early eighties, many had to cope with the introduction of computing and of computers. They may also be expected to share general advisory duties with colleagues in relation to a number of local schools. This may involve acting as a sounding board for a local head and in recent times the difficult diplomatic exercise relating to redeployment. In addition to specific and regular duties, the adviser is probably endeavouring at any one time to concentrate on particular development activities, e.g. producing curriculum guidelines, encouraging the use of computers in the mathematics classroom.

Unless there is a major crisis, therefore, the adviser is unlikely to make frequent contact with a particular maths department. It will require the initiative of the head of department to establish a relationship which will maximise the benefit of the adviser's services. It may be valuable to tap the adviser's:

i) awareness of courses, materials, methodology and people in the area, with considerable opportunity for learning from others
ii) knowledge of regional and national developments and activities
iii) experience of ways of dealing with personnel management issues – e.g. incompetent staff member, excessive expectations from head
iv) necessary involvement in assessing competence of a probationary teacher, particularly if extended probation or failure are envisaged
v) capacity for being a consultant in relation to planned curriculum development and in-service activity
vi) advocacy in supporting head of department's ideas to his head teacher
vii) control over additional resources for development work and approval for attending in-service courses with LEA support
viii) role in establishing working groups, HoD seminars, meetings and other local initiatives which may be professionally interesting and indirectly useful to the department.

Following DES initiatives, in 1985 many authorities have substantially increased advisory services in mathematics. These may be advisory teachers who should be free of administrative duties and therefore able to work with teachers in classrooms. Such a development providing both expertise and increased person power, offers opportunities for initiatives by heads of departments in developing school-based in-service training. If we are to maximise the benefit to our department, we shall probably need to take this initiative.

5) HMIs

The number of inspectors with a mathematics specialism was increased in the period following publication of the Cockcroft Report. While spending much of their time visiting and reporting on the work in schools, colleges and training institutions, they may also have a particular expertise within mathematics (e.g. statistics, computing) and may be involved in organising regional and national courses. A visit from the inspectorate can be seen as an ordeal, but it does have potential for useful professional interchange. It is worth inquiring if there is a mathematics HMI based in the locality as a first stage to establishing contact.

Other departments

1) *IN GENERAL*

A teacher's pastoral role, other teaching and extra-curricular activities inevitably lead to a network of contacts throughout the school. However, experience suggests that a large department with a well established base can be in danger of weakening its links with other parts of the school. It seems important to establish a departmental stance which recognises and has some understanding of the interrelated contributions of parts of the curriculum. We have a particularly important part to play in this, both at a decision making level with senior staff and at an interpretation level when engaged in departmental discussions. Departmental autonomy and pride have their place but it is hoped that pupils are receiving a packaged curriculum which consists of harmonious parts!

Since schools differ considerably, it may well be that other HoD colleagues in a school share an understanding of the issues and problems which the maths HoD is currently facing. Communication at this level is perhaps under-used as a result of long standing departmental insularity.

2) *MATHEMATICS RELATED DEPARTMENTS*

Mathematics is inevitably regarded as a service subject by many people. Physical scientists probably make the strongest demands with their expectation that students will have various techniques available to be applied in the context of science. More recently biologists and geographers have shown greater interest in using mathematical notation, forms of representation and some techniques, particularly those of modelling and probability and statistics. Teachers in these subjects, often with modest attainments themselves in mathematics, usually seem to make more tentative overtures and enable a more productive dialogue to be established. Physicists and chemists who have a firm knowledge of applied mathematics themselves, may be impatient with other emphases in mathematics teaching and be unconvinced by arguments about the conceptual difficulty of certain mathematical ideas for lower secondary pupils. They may decide to cut their losses in relation to depending on mathematics taught by the mathematics department and apply one or both of the following strategies:

a) minimise the amount of mathematics used
b) present the mathematical techniques required themselves.

Such a state of affairs may resolve the problem in the teachers' minds but hardly that of the pupils' experience!

The problem of establishing better communication seems to have been with teachers of mathematics and science a long time. The Mathematical Association established a working group which unearthed much material of mutual interest but few long standing examples of effective working. Initial discussions were common. Lists of terminology and techniques were drawn up and sequenced, disagreements over timing and teaching methodology were identified. Appendix 6.1 shows a preliminary checklist of children's mathematical capabilities from the science department. Communicating these findings and/or agreements through two large departments was difficult. Maintaining the dialogue was also problematic and as it often operated at an analytic level and not at a classroom teaching level, its impact on the pupils' experience is uncertain.

One promising approach was to encourage maths and science teachers to work together on occasions. Listening to the way scientists use mathematics with their classes is more revealing than much describing of 'what I do'. Sharing a field trip or a laboratory exercise is likely to give valuable insights into how the 'other mind' works and also, perhaps, to modify the examples used in mathematics and the mathematical techniques used in science.

In summary, the problem is a major one which requires considerable time and commitment if it is to be eased. Four parallel kinds of activity seem desirable:

i) Awareness of various reports, listings and cross-subject materials which could well be available in the department library (see Appendix 7 for a listing)
ii) Preparation of appropriate documentation which
   - informs other departments about timing and content of related work
   - indicates particular needs and problems which might have to be lived with or resolved in curricular revision.
iii) Opportunities for joint working, in order to
   - increase awareness
   - share problem solving rather than apportioning blame
   - lead to modifications in curriculum and teaching.
iv) Appoint a member of the department to be responsible for developing a more effective working relationship.

Other services within the school

It hardly needs stating that support services for secondary teachers are often very inadequate. Differing patterns which exist often represent accidents of history rather than obvious rational planning. Good personal relationships would seem to be the key to maximising benefits from a given situation. Teachers being by status and salary more highly placed need to take the initiative in establishing good relations. Consider the checklist in Table 6.2 in relation to people from whom help may be forthcoming.

Secretaries	• Do they have the facilities and/or knowledge to cope with the particular demands of typing and drawing needed in mathematics?
Technicians	• Almost certainly the preserve of science and CDT. Are relations good enough to secure occasional help – e.g. in supply and use of equipment?
Resource Centre	• Meeting the demands of a large staff can easily lead to a bureaucratic approach on the part of the service. Can those operating the service be helped to feel they are part of the teaching/learning enterprise of the school? Are members of the department briefed/monitored to avoid negative attitudes developing through abuses of the system?
Caretakers, Cleaners, Groundsmen	• What level of communication exists between head of department and the caretaker and those who clean the maths rooms? Are there particular problems associated with the rooms which can be eased by awareness and consultation?

TABLE 6.2

Other schools

Aspects of this issue have been considered earlier in this booklet so at this point only a check list is provided. Internal demands on staff in a school can lead to insularity. While some contacts may lead to additional work (e.g. establishing a strong link with feeder schools), others may prove useful as sources of ideas, advice and materials.

The listing in Table 6.3 overleaf might form a starting point for examining local practice in relation to contacts between our maths department and other departments and institutions who have worked or will work with the same pupils.

Type of School/ College	Activity
Feeder Primary	• Visits from final year pupils. Allot a mathematics link teacher to each major feeder school. Visits by official 'link' staff and other teachers. Joint maths staff meetings. Reporting back on pupils - Year 1, 5, 7?
Local Secondary	• Sharing information on staff and their specialisms, on courses, books, exams used. Joint staff meetings on common problems or on activities/experience specific to one school. Heads of department meeting - at local as well as at county level.
Local Independent/ other Compre-hensive (in an adjacent authority)	• Interchange of information, visits, exchange of staff. Initiative particularly important since communication networks may be parochial, e.g. within a county, between independent schools, etc.
Local FE	• Information on staff and particular expertise - also facilities, resources, communication about pupils who leave school for the college.

TABLE 6.3

Parents

It is generally recognised that the home background is a major determinant of a child's performance at school. Parents represent a significant teaching force for certain purposes; we need their help. Yet, regrettably, many parents consider themselves to have been failures in mathematics. They are likely to interpret their child's mathematical education through their own experiences while at school. What are the implications of this for the department?

There is a need to provide information, and advice of two distinct kinds:

a) the maths curriculum in general
b) the progress of an individual pupil in particular.

This information service will be a continuing one through the years, both in relation to a pupil passing through the school, and for succeeding year groups. With a changing staff in a large department, a departmental policy and a written statement of it seem desirable. Since the successful implementation of the policy will depend on it being understood and supported by each member of the department, it seems best for the policy to emerge as a result of departmental discussions.

Towards this end, the MA publication *Sharing Mathematics with Parents* (1987) and the SMP In-service Resource Kit *Communicating with Parents* may be found helpful. The latter contains an identification of issues, and case studies of practices in some schools including descriptions of maths evenings for parents. There are activities to stimulate thinking within the department and to assist in the development of necessary reporting and consultation skills. The Table 6.4 on the opposite page may be found helpful as a structured check list for thinking about the ways - intended and otherwise - that parents learn about mathematics for their child in your department!

<table>
<tr><td colspan="2">Formal information provision</td><td>Informal information available</td></tr>
<tr><td>In General
Information on
• Curriculum
• Equipment
• Organisation
• Performance in external exams
• Extra curricular activities</td><td>Relating to Individual Pupil
Reports on progress
Consultation about course choices, remedial, extension work</td><td>Homework
• textbooks
• exercise books
• help required
Supper time stories
Other parents</td></tr>
<tr><td>Form in which provided
Prospectus
Background papers
Letters
Option evenings
Subject presentations</td><td>Form of Communication
Oral
Written reports
Special interviews</td><td></td></tr>
</table>

TABLE 6.4

From a review of present practice and of needs, there may emerge a clearer policy and the need for certain identified skills to be developed by members of the department. For example, some simulated parent interviews may be a stimulating way to face appropriate issues. The MA booklet *Starting as a Mathematics Teacher* contains practical advice on meeting parents for probationary teachers.

Employers

In considering links betwen schools and employers it is easy for the discussion to become polarised and for participants to become defensive about their own position. It would seem that over the last decade, debate and consultation have led to a greater understanding of the inherent problems and to an increase in mutual respect. Nevertheless major problems still exist, for example:

i) employers looking for particular skills, adopt a different standpoint from those charged with the responsibility of providing a general education
ii) different employers require different skills
iii) grades in public examinations do not specify what a young person can do
iv) employers appear less critical of the mathematical competence of the more able entrants, regardless of the non-specified skills
v) most 16-year-old leavers are not going directly into employment
vi) most teachers have not been employed for any substantial period outside the education system

vii) employers are unclear about the mathematical demands made on young entrants. Entrance tests are often of limited arithmetic skills rather than presenting problems in the context in which they will be met by employees.

In the light of the complexity of the situation at this interface, the Cockcroft Committee (para 100) stated that 'It must be a primary aim of liaison to enable schools and employers to obtain a better understanding of each others' needs and problems and of the way in which each operates.' Most departments have probably made only limited progress in establishing an appropriate level of liaison. Some developments worth considering are as follows:

Exploring ways of communicating more clearly to those outside the education system, what a young person is able to do.
During the last ten years a large number of numeracy schemes and certificates have been developed. Some are specific to a particular school, others have been used widely. Some of these schemes have focused narrowly on arithmetic skills, most encounter the danger of developing long lists of skills which can either lead to some form of indigestion in the reader or require some form of aggregation to lead to statements of the form – 'scored more than 75 per cent on a test covering the items listed'. As all forms of record keeping show, it is one thing to design and complete detailed forms, it is quite another to know if the recipient (a) wishes and (b) is able to interpret the report.

One of the most substantial systematic studies, is that being carried out into graduated assessment by a team involving personnel from Suffolk Education Authority, the SMP and Chelsea College. This scheme has been operating for over five years. In this time the scheme has been developed, implemented and evaluated. The last stage involves a thorough study of the use actually made of the data by employers. The use of grade related criteria in a second phase of the development of GCSE, is a move on a national scale to provide a clearer statement of outcomes from the national examination system.

Achieving greater awareness of how mathematics is used in various kinds of work.
Again, there is a two part problem. First, finding out what is used and second, finding ways to incorporate appropriate examples and approaches in our teaching. The first has turned out to be more difficult than was first imagined. The most fruitful progress has been made by a mathematics educator observing people at work, talking with them and their supervisors and distilling the nature of the activity in relation to mathematics. Fitzgerald's work in providing evidence for the Cockcroft Committee has advanced the art considerably and has led subsequently to the development of teaching materials and a television series. The latter may make an important contribution to the second problem of enabling us as teachers to incorporate ideas, approaches and examples into our teaching programme where appropriate.

Hopefully initiatives of this kind can assist liaison between a school and its local employers. Nevertheless it requires considerable willpower and time to make significant progress and the immediate demands of within school issues threaten the liaison movement with being a minority interest. A member of a department with a particular interest or expertise may well help a department to keep working at this.

Using pupil experiences as a starting point for some mathematical activity.
With work experience in years 3 to 5 becoming more common, there may well be opportunities to examine 'maths at work' in a variety of contexts. If links with some companies are regular then some preparatory work both with the company and with the pupils may greatly enhance what can be achieved in post-experience activity.

Organising staff attachments to companies.
Such an experience could be significant in helping teachers to get a feel for the employees' and employers' perspective. Achieving a balance between breadth of experience in several work situations and substantial experience in one will not be easy. For many, the benefit of such involvement may be maximised if carried out in collaboration with a training institution or a teachers' centre. This may help (a) in reflecting on and evaluating the experiences, (b) in sharing the experiences with others who have been in different work situations and (c) in thinking about the implications for the department and for one's own teaching.

Involving local employers where appropriate and possible in some parts of the teaching programme.
This may involve only a few visitors attending and contributing to a small number of lessons in a year. Nevertheless it would be indicative of greater openness and might form a growth point for a variety of activities.

Encourage financial and/or moral (named) sponsorship by industry and commerce of mathematics initiatives.
The potential for this is likely to be affected by geographical and commercial/industrial circumstances. An original idea may well catch the imagination of a local company and of Rotary. Support may be found for organising quizzes, problem solving competitions etc. The experience of some schools when given outmoded computer equipment in the seventies should be an encouragement to be careful about responding to some kinds of generosity.

Exploring the way in which mathematics in work is projected through careers literature convention.
Discussion with the careers teacher and possibly links with other parts of the careers service may help to develop awareness in this area.

Training institutions

1) *INITIAL TRAINING*

Training for mathematics teaching is currently offered in polytechnics, colleges of higher education and in universities. Each institution currently has an agreed number of places for training in mathematics. Since January 1984, mathematics and science graduates, who were formerly exempt from the requirement to obtain a Postgraduate Certificate in Education have had to obtain the teaching qualification to gain qualified teacher status. This requirement now applies to anyone who graduated in these subjects after the original requirement for graduates in general was introduced in 1973.

Training may take one of the following forms:

a) one year Postgraduate Certificate in Education courses (about 700 entrants in 1985).
b) undergraduate courses (about 280 entrants in 1985)
   - 3/4 year B.Ed. course specialising in mathematics
   - 4 year concurrent degree and teaching certificate course.

In 1984 the Secretary of State established a Council for the Accreditation of Teacher Education (CATE) to be responsible for approving course proposals which would be required to meet specified criteria (see Appendix 6.2). For example, PGCE courses are now required to be of at least 36 weeks in length and at least 15 of those weeks must be spent in school-based work.

Many training institutions have sought to develop a partnership with experienced teachers in schools in preparing new entrants to teaching. At its best, the contribution of the experienced teachers provides teaching experience, advice and resources within a school department and complements the work of the tutors whose distance from the day to day work of the classroom enables them to help students explore different approaches/possibilities and introduces them to current thinking, materials and practice.

If there is a training institution not too far from the school, there is probably a tradition of offering a place (or refusing same) to a mathematics student. Although it will make demands on the staff, the contact with raw new graduates (and some maturer entrants to the profession) can be stimulating and worthwhile.

2) *IN-SERVICE TRAINING*

Training institutions provide one source of in-service training. School-based training, local authority courses, HMI courses, OU courses and MA and ATM conferences are other substantial means of further professional training. There is little cohesion, direction or completeness about what is on offer within a region of the country, let alone in a smaller area. Enthusiastic individuals, interested pressure groups and aware officers promote a whole variety of activities. Teachers who are prepared to give up time and to pay a significant proportion of the cost, can avail themselves of what is on offer.

The system has the advantages of flexibility, responsiveness and freedom for the individual teacher and the provider. However, its fragmented and under-resourced nature has not encouraged a professional expectation of further training, both academic and practical, as a normal part of the life of a mathematics teacher. Developments in the last few years suggest that this situation is changing and we are likely, as HoDs, to be more involved in encouraging and contributing to various kinds of provision. GRIST funding and Local Financial Management seem likely to cause major changes within the immediate future.

It is certainly in the interests of heads of department to acquaint themselves with the people and the provision in their locality. Training institutions carry a substantial collection of books, teaching materials, journals and other resources of interest to subject teachers. While primarily for the use of currently enrolled students, they may well be accessible to other teachers in the area. It is certainly worth enquiring.

Examination boards

In our experience, teachers become involved in the work of the public examination system for a variety of reasons. They may intend:

i) to deepen their understanding of the examination process in order to improve their teaching of examination classes
ii) to exert influence on the development of systems (both structure and content) in order to reflect what they see to be desirable aims in the teaching of mathematics
iii) to gain professional status and power at the point which determines much of what happens in secondary schools
iv) to supplement their earnings.

In the GCE system, teachers were most likely to have been involved in the marking of scripts. The design, development and application of a marking scheme while working alongside a group of largely unknown fellow professionals can be illuminating, leading to a greater awareness of issues and to the development of skills. The systems of moderation, the generosity of the faceless examiner and the fallibility of the human marker may all be enlightening to the newly appointed examiner faced with the rituals developed by the long experienced 'professionals'. The experience of participating in such an exercise can be a useful departmental resouce in sharpening up the preparation of examination candidates. From their introduction in 1965, the CSE examinations involved a much higher degree of teacher participation. While Mode 1 offered similar opportunities to GCE for 'faceless' marking, the Mode 3 system has involved the development of examination syllabuses, the preparation of marking schemes and often the marking of scripts by teachers in their own school.

Most examination boards have a structure of subject committees which advise them on syllabuses, assessment techniques and on the effectiveness of the examination papers and marking schemes, as well as on the proper functioning of the marking and grading systems. A chief examiner, a moderator and a team of markers will be appointed – the actual structure varying somewhat between boards. The subject committee will be responsible for several examinations in the subject field and over a period of time develops an expertise in monitoring standards and in implementing new features of a system – syllabus changes, assessment techniques etc. The examination world appears to be a distinct sub-culture of the teaching profession. Those appointed to senior positions in it have often served a long apprenticeship as markers and as members of committees. Vital to the smooth working of a system using the part-time contribution of teachers and lecturers is the work of the examination board officers. The person responsible for the mathematics examinations may well have a background in mathematics teaching but the major task will be to co-ordinate the contributions of the part-time subject specialists.

The arrival of the GCSE brought some uncertainties about the role of teachers in the public examination system. The increased central control exercised by the Secondary Examinations Council through the five examination groups might suggest an increase in distance between classroom teacher and external examiner, but the need for the assessment of project work and oral skills suggests that we shall be involved in a substantial part of the 16+ assessment system within our department.

Many teachers may feel excluded from the examination process by its distant operation and its necessarily formal administrative style. Groups like the MEI (Mathematics in Education and Industry) have deliberately set out to encourage participation in syllabus development and the review of results; this has achieved a fairly unusual high level of teacher involvement. For the persistent teacher, who is keen to become involved, responding to advertisements for examiners or direct contact with examination boards can lead to the first point of entry to this crucially influential activity within the education system.

Teachers' centres

The pattern of provision appears to differ from county to county. Some authorities have a single substantial centre serving all their teachers. In other places there are several centres with some specialising in mathematics. The relevance of a teachers' centre to a head of department's work may depend on its geographical location and on the kinds of expertise and facilities which the centre can offer. In many areas primary school teachers seem to make greater use of such centres but establishing contact with the warden and enquiring about resources and facilities seem potentially worthwhile exercises for a HoD. It may well provide a congenial and 'neutral' professional meeting point for a departmental in-service day or a meeting with colleagues from other schools.

Professional associations

Professional associations have been formed when individuals have felt the need to benefit from each other's expertise both from meeting each other and from communication in written form. It is often a particular concern within their professional life which acts as a launch pad for a new association with the belief that their corporate voice will be more effective in representing their interests and perhaps achieving particular ends.

Mathematics teachers have the advantage (or the problem) of having two substantial associations. The Mathematical Association, founded in 1871 with a concern for the improvement of geometry teaching, had its roots in the independent and grammar schools. In the last 20 years its widening concerns are reflected in regular publications for primary teachers and for those teaching secondary pupils across the ability range. For many years it has produced occasional reports which have been informative and influential. The oldest and mathematically most sophisticated journal *The Mathematical Gazette* continues to carry the most thorough and substantial reviews of books which are relevant to teachers of mathematics. In recent years working groups have been established to prepare specific reports or handbooks. The annual conference at Easter and occasional weekend conferences provide national meeting points to supplement meetings organised by local branches. The Association has its administrative base in Leicester (259 London Road LE2 3BE) and an extensive library which is housed in the University of Leicester.

The Association of Teachers of Mathematics was formed in 1952. It also had a particular focus initially with its concern about the use of aids to communicate mathematical ideas. It has always adopted a more radical stance than the older association and has produced a valuable counter image, a fund of teaching ideas, a concern for the processes of learning and teaching mathematics and free wheeling vitality that makes it both attractive and at times contentious. It has encouraged open-ended mathematical activity with its publications and through its local meetings and annual conferences. It has provided a point of contact and an avenue of communication for some very imaginative teachers and creative mathematics educators. Its administrative base is in Derby (7 Shaftesbury Street, DE3 8YB).

It can be argued that every teacher of mathematics should be a member of at least one of these associations providing as they do a stimulus, a broader view of the work of the mathematics teacher and a continuous updating on current issues and developments. Copies of their reports and perhaps their journals should well be a valued part of a departmental library. As HoDs we might well provide the stimulus to greater involvement in local and national activities.

Other professionally relevant associations of which it may be useful to be aware are:

> The Institute of Mathematics and its Applications - the professional body for mathematicians which has an education section.
>
> The National Association of Mathematics Advisers - association for LEA advisers and inspectors.
>
> The National Association of Teachers in Higher and Further Education - the mathematics section caters for lecturers in colleges of education, F E and polytechnics.
>
> The Association of University Mathematics Education Teachers - providing for mathematics tutors in university education departments.

Representatives from the last three mentioned together with those from the MA and the ATM meet as a body called the Standing Committee of Associations concerned with Mathematics Education in Schools (SCAMES) to discuss matters of mutual concern and in particular to make representation on behalf of mathematics educationalists. The body was initially particularly active in commenting on the draft criteria for the GCSE examinations in mathematics.

Conclusion

The majority of both teachers and the general public seem likely to agree that the current trend away from the insular classroom is to be welcomed. For those who have the time and opportunity to look around, it is striking to see how the amount of literature and activity relating to mathematics education has increased. Several universities and other institutions of higher education have established mathematics education centres with a resulting focusing of interests and an output of development and research material. At a local level, development and in-service activity and the work of advisory teachers provides another dimension.

To those of us attempting to run a department, the agenda presented by this chapter may be more daunting than exhilarating. To start on some areas which seem particularly relevant to our current situation seems most appropriate. Opportunities to consult with other HoDs engaged on similar tasks will offer stimulus and encouragement, ideas and experience, together with a valuable reminder that while schools may have much in common, their traditions and current concerns may provide very different perspectives on life beyond the department.

Postscript

Meeting of a publications committee of the Mathematical Association

Professor A F Fable:	University mathematician and Chairman
Mr A Round:	Head of Department
Dr A Star:	College Tutor
Ms A Ware:	Teacher
Mr C Hall:	Adviser
Mr M Etal	Executive Secretary

Professor Fable: I trust everyone has had a chance to read this handbook which people keep saying is much in demand. Certainly the gestation period has been long enough. Our task is to decide whether it's fit to publish!

Mr Round: It's given me a few sleepless nights and it took all my wife's powers of persuasion to stop me from resigning and returning to the back-benches. Admittedly I read it right through at two sittings but the implications for a HoD like me in my mid fifties are frankly disturbing. We already do many of the things recommended but the list of potential activities seems endless. Perhaps the younger generation will take it more in their stride. Certainly there's plenty to help a new HoD avoid some of the costly mistakes I made. The focus on the pupil's viewpoint stopped me in my tracks – all too easy to forget in coping with the demands of the system.

Mr Hall: If I could get all my HoDs to take this on board it would be a major step forward. We thought of following Leicestershire and Hertfordshire's example and writing our own handbook but there never seems enough time. It might be worth us writing an Exshire supplement to this one to cover local circumstances. I shall certainly make sure there's a copy in every secondary school – it will form a good starting point for discussion when I visit the school and talk with the HoD and the headteacher.

Dr Star: The authors must attend some of the conferences I go to! Plenty of good ideas and some quite extraordinary assumptions and generalisations – but they are entitled to their view I guess, even in an Association publication! My chief worry is that it will be just another worthy report to be added to the HoD's overloaded shelf. Unless time is provided for analysis, reflection and application, I can see that there will be very little implementaion. Those on HoD courses may have the best opportunity to digest its contents. Perhaps informal study groups at colleges and teachers' centres might be an immediate help.

Ms Ware: I found it interesting as I am thinking about applying for HoD posts. One worry I have is that because there is so much change in maths education, I think the book may quickly become dated. Already the information on GCSE looks thin. I notice that all the committee members were male; this probably explains the emphasis at times!

Mr Etal: It's a substantial publication and, beyond our known membership, it is difficult to predict the number of orders. It will represent a considerable outlay if we are to publish using an outside printer. We shall need to clear it with the treasurer.

Professor Fable: The reactions seem generally positive and I would concur. Our individual detailed comments and suggestions can be passed through to the writing group for their final revision. My lingering concern is about who is the intended reader – will the new boy make much of it and will the old experienced school-master bother to read it?

Ms Ware: Some of the oft forgotten women in the profession might!

Dr Star: There are several targets to be hit and the tone is such as to involve all the ones I'm aware of.

Professor Fable: So we authorise? Publish and be damned?

Mr Hall: Yes; in all probability we shall.

Mr Round: I did have some doubts about the Postscript.

Professor Fable: Now what about the other publication, *Teaching Mathematics in the 1990s?*

Appendix 1: Reflections of experience as a head of department

'Leaving?' by Peter Stockwell (*Mathematics Teaching* No. 120, Sept. 1987)

Department of Education, Loughborough University of Technology. (Head of Mathematics at Montsaye School in Northamptonshire until 31.12.86)

It took six head of department interviews before I was matched with a suitable school. Like most people I do not relish the interview situation, and I came from the first two knowing I had not been placed (let alone finishing second as a remarkable number of interviewees do!). It was not easy to accept how the intensity of the situation could make me so nervous and incapable of putting over my views in a clear and succinct manner. It helped when I started concentrating on what I wanted to say and not on what I thought they wanted to hear. The next two interviews were at schools I did not want to work in, and I withdrew. Penultimately I felt I had performed reasonably well, and I did not get the job. Finally I found myself and five others in a mixed eleven to eighteen comprehensive school that we all liked. I'm sure the long day and five o'clock interview were the main reasons for my success. By that time there was no tension left, I must have been as close to my 'usual self' as I am ever likely to be on interview.

Like most new heads of department, I had definite views as to what needed to be done. Courses were wrong, groupings incorrect, resources poor, environment depressing, textbooks and teaching materials out of date, furniture in need of replacement. The teaching itself, however, seemed of a good standard. Six years on I feel the need to replace 'I' by 'we' and we have had some success in achieving the above objectives. The changes took a lot of time, effort and hardwork from the teachers in the department and help, understanding and assistance from those with power, and money, outside the department. My successor as head of department will be able to assess the situation and come to the conclusion that, courses are wrong, groupings incorrect, resources poor, ...! Some investigation in terms of continuity and the frequency and purpose of changes of departmental heads would seem overdue.

On reflection, all the important aspects and lasting impressions are to do with feelings and emotions. To this day I can clearly remember my personal dislike of the job during the first term. I craved to be back in the security of my former department, where I was known and, I hope, respected, where somebody else was the 'front man' and where I could happily choose where to make my input to departmental affairs. My own insecurities were immediately revealed on encountering pupils who did not cooperate. Of course I knew all the stories about how hard it was to establish oneself in a new school. This did not help much when I knew how vital it was to be seen immediately as 'a good teacher' by my departmental colleagues. It helped when the lady teacher next door informed me how much quieter they were with me than the previous teacher, it helped more to discover that I had been given some of the most difficult groups in years three and four although no one had told me. Undoubtedly my major concern in the first term was establishing myself as a credible classroom teacher, in my own eyes, and hopefully in those of others. I still suspect this aspect is initially overlooked by new staff in positions of responsibility, particularly the extra classroom pressure that the position of responsibility brings.

My next main memory from the early days is just what a difficult job it is. It never became easy, of course, but there were times when I wondered if it was a viable job for one individual. This is a point that still causes me unease. Given the high teaching load that heads of department carry and that most are required, or wish to be tutors, where do they find the time to teach their lessons in a satisfactory, or better, manner and attend to the multitude of other tasks that occur in the short, medium and long term? I do not wish to produce a list here but, without exception, they are many, varied, time consuming and continually present. Many are routine, but still have to be done and consume valuable time. The easiest to avoid are the most important and time consuming. These involve dealing with, and providing support for, people (colleagues and children). In my experience it is fellow mathematics teachers who do not receive the time and attention they deserve and this must be the most serious omission of all. In trying to create time for this I found myself under pressure to deal with more routine, administrative matters at odd moments of the day; this then starts to happen at odd moments during lessons and very soon teaching and pupils are suffering. This pressure is increasing for many heads of departments in that it coincides with a time of growing commitment and involvement with one's own family.

Unfortunately, I know of no solution to this dilemma. It impinges on what became, for me, the centre piece of the head of department's role. Perhaps it is more so in a shortage subject than others that the head of department has a crucial role in providing support and assisting in the development of his subject teaching colleagues. I gradually became aware that this was more fundamental than which teaching material or syllabus detail was under review. My contacts with other heads of departments and mathematics teachers inclines me to the view that this is not believed by many others. Lip-service may be paid to this support role but to be effective it is time consuming and under-pins all other development work. It requires a person approach to the teaching and learning of mathematics rather than a content or methodology approach. Content and methodology are important but subsidiary to the person approach.

Despite the very real difficulties outlined above I was fortunate in having a second in department who was capable and willing to shoulder large amounts of content and method work, particularly in revision of courses and induction of new teachers. She also made major contributions to administrative work and gave her own, distinctive contribution to the development of a person approach. Such an approach is not new or clever or difficult or unique. It simply stems from a belief that mathematics learning can only become effective if teacher and taught engage in the task in a willing and cooperative manner. Much time and research is devoted to the creation of these conditions for the learner. It is often taken for granted that teachers approach their lessons in this manner, it is frequently not the case. It is a desire to produce such a situation through the sharing of common aims and objectives, taking time to deal with each other's concerns and problems, realising that all teachers need some type of professional development (varied though that might be), that produces a person approach and consumes huge amounts of time.

It was this change of emphasis that remains as the major factor in my time as a head of mathematics, not least because of the rewards and benefits such an approach brought to me in terms of relationships within the department.

There are a multitude of individual incidents that remain clearly in the memory, many of these are basic to working with children and not directly the result of being a head of department. The repeated high A-level uptake is rewarding but off-set by the minority involvement of girls; despite a majority of female mathematics teachers. We have tried to take positive measures to remedy the problem but it is hard to combat the views of society at large and parents and peers in particular. If the measures and policies adopted have any effect it will be in future years; I suspect attitudes are developed at a very early age (pre-school?). How many daughters receive technic Lego™ sets for birthdays or Christmas?

'Maths, Magic and the Moon' was a production given at the school by a group of professional actors. Promoted and organised by the second in department its effect across the school was out of all proportion to the production itself (which was excellent). Was this really the mathematics department booking the school hall for a major dramatic production, requesting disruption to the timetable, working in conjunction with the drama department? Not only did such events take place but the pupils paid money to watch and participate in something with 'Maths' in the title! That it was over subscribed and caused such a positive stir within the school surely points the way forward to other activities. Participation in, and winning, the county mathematics quiz gave great joy to the younger, ablest mathematicians as did personal guidance and concern for the mathematical learning programmes of the most able, older pupils. I have become convinced that the promotion of special activities as frequently as possible mixed with concern for individual progress in mathematics learning will do more to enhance mathematical attitudes than years of tinkering and changing syllabuses.

Conclusions? I always felt that I had done a full day's work. It is not a job I would want to do until retirement but it is not an experience I would have wanted to miss. It was very demanding and very rewarding. We were eight full time teachers of mathematics; we could have done a really thorough job with ten teachers but I suppose a 25 percent increase is what the profession needs in virtually all aspects.

Appendix 2.1: Purpose, aims and objectives in teaching mathematics

An extract from *Journey into Mathematics Teachers' Guide 1* by A. Bell, A. Wigley and D. Rooke (Blackie, 1978), p. 2

WHY TEACH MATHEMATICS?

Mathematics is a characteristic way of organising our experience of the world which is employed wherever there is a 'pattern' or 'structure'. As such it may enrich our understanding, enabling us to relate and interpret our experiences as well as giving pleasure. As a subject, therefore, it lies at the heart of a great deal of human activity.

Mathematics has important applications in many other fields, for example science, engineering, social sciences and management. We cannot say what mathematical knowledge will be useful to our students, but a significant proportion will need to know some mathematics and also be aware of how it can be applied.

Mathematics provides the most readily accessible form of problem solving in the classroom because it does not depend on the pre-existence of a substantial body of knowledge. Involvement in problem solving enables pupils to exercise and acquire confidence in their intellectual powers. Thinking independently and expressing arguments in a logical and ordered manner does not always come easily. Good habits can be acquired by being in an environment in which thinking is explicitly valued, and by coming to recognise the general value of reasoning. One may also acquire some strategies which are more generally useful.

COMPONENTS OF MATHEMATICAL LEARNING

A complex human activity like mathematics comprises a number of components of dissimilar natures. In turning this activity into a part of the school curriculum, it is necessary to identify these components so as to ensure that a suitably balanced combination of them is chosen, and because they may require different teaching methods. The division we shall make is into:

i) concepts and relationships
ii) skills and facts
iii) strategies
iv) attitudes.

The most characteristic self-justifying activity in mathematics is problem solving in its various aspects – firstly, searching for patterns, and secondly applying to practical problems and situations. Problem solving is the end to which the learning of a particular content (concepts, skills, etc.) is the means. Although there has been some shift of emphasis in mathematics courses away from 'skills' and towards 'concepts', in many cases 'content' objectives have still predominated over 'process' objectives, with creative activity often being neglected. The balanced course which we seek tries to take account of motivation towards doing mathematics, and also to measure up to the reasons which have been given to justify the subject as a compulsory element of the curriculum.

The aims of mathematics teaching as discussed in *Mathematics from 5 to 16* (HMSO, 1985)

Mathematics as an essential element of communication
Mathematics as a powerful tool
Appreciation of relationships within mathematics
Awareness of the fascination of mathematics
Imagination, initiative and flexibility of mind in mathematics
Working in a systematic way
Working independently
Working cooperatively
In-depth study in mathematics
Pupils' confidence in their mathematical abilities

Rationale and aims within a school mathematics department – an extract from *Henry Smith School Departmental Handbook* (1982)

Any reasonable school mathematics course contains elements of both 'pure' and 'applied' mathematics. The many different syllabuses and courses, and the 'traditional v. modern' argument, simply reflect differences of opinion as to the proper point of balance between these two aspects of mathematics.

In 'pure' mathematics, as the word is used here, we are concerned with the study of mathematics as an academic discipline in its own right, without regard to any practical applications it may or may not have. Such a study may be justified by saying that it forms part of the traditional curriculum of the 'educated man', alongside literature, music, and so on. Perhaps more importantly, however, it may lead to certain 'spin-off' benefits, such as the ability to reason clearly and logically, the ability to identify and extend patterns, the ability to approach problems systematically, and the ability to follow instructions.

'Applied' mathematics, on the other hand, is concerned more with the imparting of knowledge and skills directly relevant to the pupils' present or future lives. This includes as a subset the group of skills generally known as 'numeracy' or 'survival mathematics', but it also includes the mathematical skills required in other school subjects and (to some extent at least) in pupils' future careers. This side of mathematics is important for all pupils, whatever their ability.

We have to ensure that our courses provide adequately for the needs of all the children. There will be some - perhaps one per cent - who plan to make their careers in mathematics. Their main need is for a thorough grounding in the concepts and principles of academic mathematics. A larger group - maybe ten or twenty per cent - will work as scientists or technicians or in some other occupation needing a battery of mathematical skills that can be applied fluently, but without any great interest in the underlying principles. And then three-quarters of the pupils, whether employed or not, will need very little serious mathematics once they have left school, but will still require certain 'survival skills'.

We may therefore state the aims of the Mathematics Department as being to ensure that each pupil on leaving school is numerate, has sufficient mathematical skills for the career of his/her choice, and will understand the mathematics likely to be encountered in daily adult life. In addition, we hope that pupils will acquire the logical abilities characteristic of the mathematician, and will develop an interest in the historical, recreational and cultural aspects of mathematics.

More specifically, we may list departmental objectives.

At the end of his/her mathematical education in this school, each pupil will be able

- to perform the basic 'numeracy' skills listed in the department handbook
- to perform the basic mathematical skills needed in his/her chosen career or for entry to higher or further mathematical education
- to reason clearly and logically, and to set out a logical argument
- to identify patterns encountered in diverse situations, and to extrapolate from these
- to approach problems systematically, choosing appropriate techniques for their solution
- to follow logical instructions clearly expressed
- to experience satisfaction in and enjoyment of his/her mathematical achievements
- to obtain any formal mathematical qualifications needed for his/her chosen career.

The department will therefore ensure that every pupil is given the opportunity of obtaining some formal qualification in mathematics or arithmetic, and that results in such examinations (considering all relevant factors) compare not unfavourably with the national average. A close working relationship will be maintained with other departments so as to ensure no conflict of methods.

Basic philosophy - an extract from *Backwell School Departmental Notes* (1983)

The philisophy of the department is that mathematics should be an active, not a passive learning of mathematics that someone else once did. By doing his own mathematics the pupil learns what 'to mathematise' means. He becomes involved, interested. He creates his own language to express the mathematisation that he is attempting, or else he uses an accepted language and hence also learns to appreciate what that language is for.

The whole course revolves around the basic idea of 'doing' mathematics. To solve a problem or explore relationships it is usually necessary to simplify the structure first of all, sometimes with the use of concrete materials, and hence make it easier to spot patterns that are necesary for a solution or proof. Having spotted the simpler patterns it is then possible to generalise and, hopefully, be able to convince others of the truth of the generalisation.

It is certainly not possible to 'do' mathematics without understanding what one is doing. Equally, it is not possible to create understanding without the will to understand. The will to understand can be encouraged by creating interest and involvement. It is very strongly our philosophy to interest and involve the pupils.

AIMS OF THE COURSE

i) To develop each pupil's mental imagery, both in number and geometry.

ii) To train each pupil to become numerate in three ways:

   a) mental arithmetic
   b) pencil and paper arithmetic
   c) using a calculator sensibly.

iii) To develop each pupil's confidence and ability to solve problems and discover relationships.

iv) To help each pupil to discover, learn and appreciate known relationships and techniques.

v) To develop each pupil's ability to use known relationships and techniques in mathematics lessons, in other subject disciplines in the school and in life outside of school.

vi) To devise and use a suitable form of assessment of each pupil's ability to achieve the above and to ensure that this assessment is beneficial to each pupil's career in further education or employment.

EXTRACT FROM A DEPARTMENTAL WORK SCHEME

YEAR ONE WORKSCHEMES
AUTUMN TERM

ORDER	TOPIC	SYLLABUS CONTENT	TEXT REFERENCES	WORKSHEETS	SOFTWARE AND OTHER RESOURCES
0	Investigations	Introduction to investigations, suggest choose from Table Square, Digit Add, Jigsaws, Handshakes, Lines and Points.		1121, 1104	Rose Circles Resources Files
1	Flow Charts	Instructions and orders, Decision boxes, Branches and loops, red/white box	MIA1 Chapter 1		
2	Numbers in Action I	Fairground, on tour, school shop, Magic squares, puzzles, sequences Out and About, making sure of + and −	MIA1 Chapter 2 MW1 Chapter 7	226 1102	Flags Autosum Dart Subgame
		HALF-TERM			
3	Statistics and graphs	Did you know? Pictographs, bar charts, collecting information	MIA1 Chapter 3 L1 Chapter 13 MW1 Chapter 16	512, 513 286, 287 516, 517	
4	Co-ordinate	X marks the spot, treasure hunts, robots, dancers Sets of points - pirates, plots, robbers, staircases	MIA1 Chapter 4 L1 Chapter 14 MW1 Chapter 8	Maggie's Booklets	Rhino Locate
5	Numbers in Action II	Sports and Pastimes Making sure of × and ÷ Out and About with numbers, puzzles	MIA1 Chapter 5 MW2 Chapter 19, 15	269, 270	Flags Autosum
6	Letters for Numbers	Introducing letters for numbers. Grouping terms Patterns (concentrate on this part) Equations (less so)	MIA1 Chapter 6 L1 Chapter 12 MW1 Chapter 11		Predict
		SPRING TERM			
7	Introducing angles	Recognising and naming angles Angles around a point Degrees and protractors. Drawing angles	MIA1 Chapter 7 L1 Chapter 8 MW1 Chapter 13	363, 364 377	Angles Angle 90 Angle 360
8	Decimals in action	+ and − × by whole number, × by decimal ÷ by whole number, rounding off a decimal Fractions and decimals. Puzzles	MIA1 Chapter 8 L1 Chapter 7 MW1 Chapter 14 MW2 Chapter 6	233, 234 265, 271 1101 283	Guess d Boxed
		HALF-TERM			
9	Tiling & Symmetry	Tiling patterns. Tessellations Line symmetry Rotational (turn) symmetry	MIA1 Chapter 9 L1 Chapter 3, 20 MW1 Chapter 17, 5	357, 381 718, 163 1111, 716	Aspire Newtiles Tilekit
10	Time and Temperature	Measuring time, calendars, 12 & 24hr. clock School, train and flight timetables TV programmes Measuring temperature	MIA1 Chapter 10 L1 Ch. 9 p. 62/63 MW1 Chapter 10 MW2 Chapter 3	254, 255, 256 263, 264 274	
		SUMMER TERM			
11	Equations	Reminder of grouping terms, Balancing Solving problems. Making sure	MIA1 Chapter 11 L1 Chapter 19 MW2 Chapter 18	113	
12	Length, area and volume	Units of length, area Area of a rectangle Units of volume Volume of a cuboid	MIA1 Chapter 12 L1 Chapter 15 L1 Ch. 11 p. 78/79 MW2 Chapter 16 MW3 Chapter 5	151, 158, 159 163, 166 160, 161 162	Workbox of nets 'Making solid models'
13	Angles again	Types of angle Horizontal and vertical Turning about a point	MIA1 Chapter 13 MW3 Chapter 1/2	see topic 7	
		HALF-TERM			
14	Saving & Spending	Earnings, expenses and saving Dining out. At the supermarket Milk delivery. On holiday	MIA1 Chapter 14 MW2 Chapter 15	 254, 255 256	Litter Taxi
15	Formulae	Finding Formulae Forming and using formulae	MIA1 Chapter 15	112	
16	Graphs and relations	Interpretation of graphs Labelling axes Plotting points	MIA1 Chapter 16		Linover Plotter

Appendix 2.2: Some ideas for implementing goal

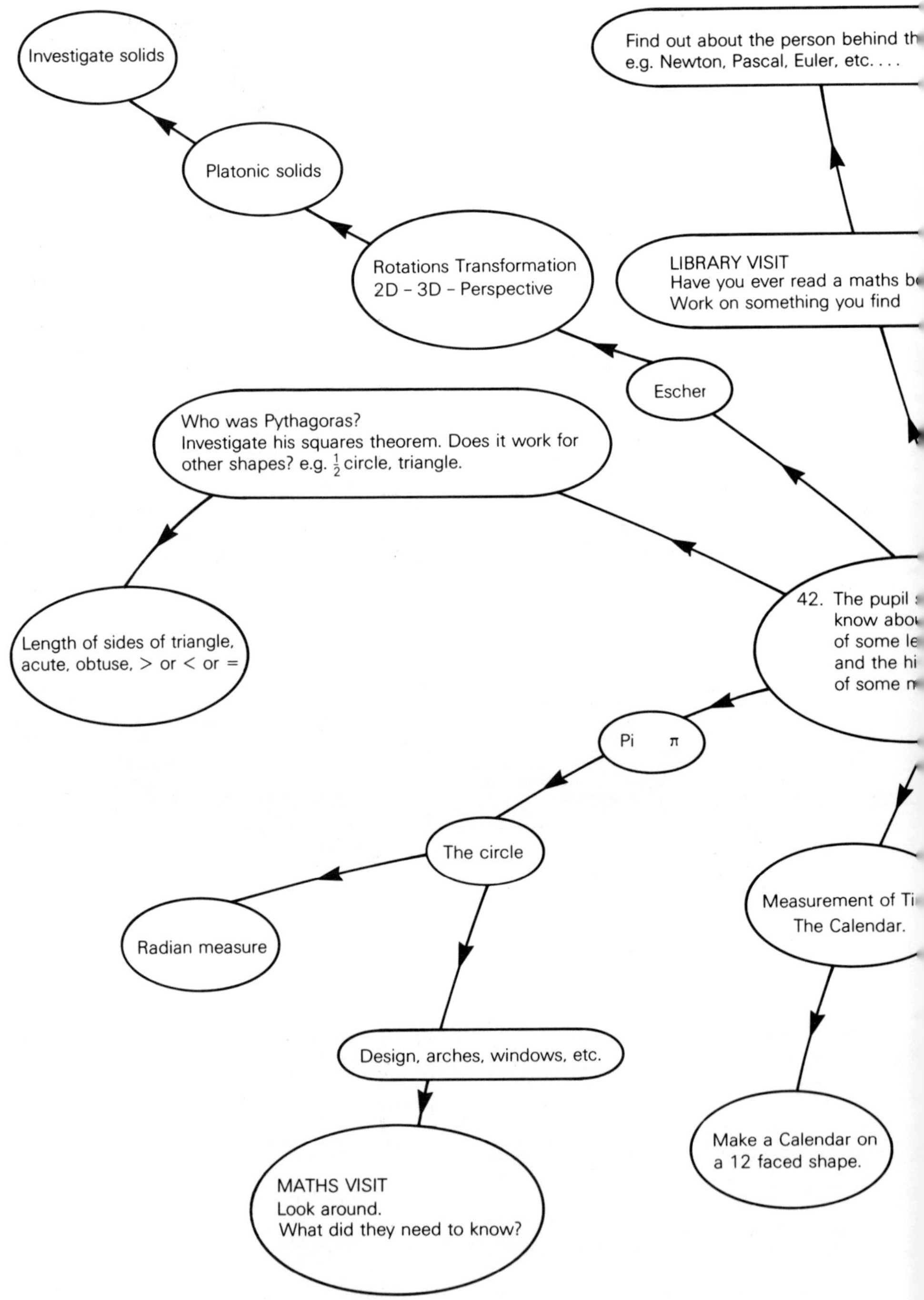

42 (*Why, What and How?* MA, 1976)

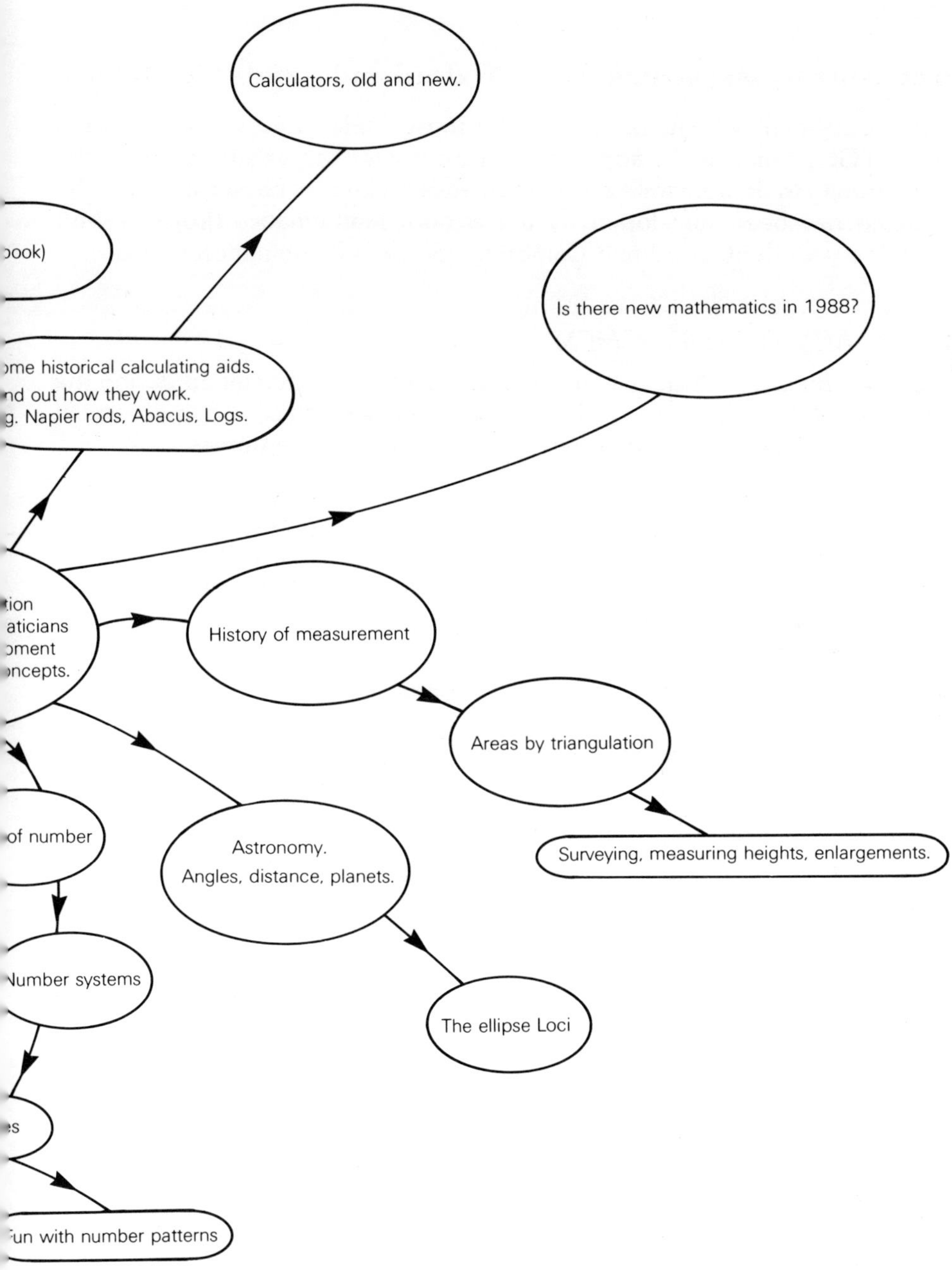

Appendix 2.3: Assessment schemes in mathematics

Graduated scheme of assessment (SMP/Oxford and Cambridge Board)

This assessment scheme is designed for those students for whom the usual style of GCSE may not be appropriate. It is designed to give such students the opportunity to demonstrate the mathematical skills they have mastered. The scheme has been developed by the School Mathematics Project (SMP) together with the Oxford and Cambridge Schools Examination Board.

SUMMARY OF THE SCHEME

Stage certificates Stages One, Two and Three may be gained during the student's 4th and 5th years. To be awarded a Stage Certificate, a student must score 70 per cent or more in each of the following seven areas:

i) *Written tests* (Recaps)
   - Using Arithmetic (arithmetical calculations in context)
   - Interpreting Data (reading graphs, 2-way tables, diagrams)
   - Applying Spatial Skills (areas, angles, scales, enlargement)
   - Interpreting 3 Dimensions (using maps, plans, views, exploded diagrams)

ii) *Mental Mathematics and Estimation tests*
iii) *Practical tests*
iv) *Oral tests of spoken communication*

Final certificate This includes a profile of the student's mathematical achievements and gives information on:
- the highest stage which the student has reached in each of the seven mathematical areas listed above
- a maximum of four pieces of individual topic work which the student has studied successfully.

Further information is available from the SMP Office, University of Southampton, Southampton SO9 5NH.

Graded Assessment in Mathematics Scheme

GAIM is one of several parallel graded assessment schemes being developed by the Inner London Education Authority (ILEA) and the University of London School Examinations Board (ULSEB) in co-operation with other bodies. The intention is to produce a mathematics assessment scheme

appropriate for all 11–16-year-old students in comprehensive schools, although it will also be suitable for many others.

GAIM will provide a detailed cumulative record of a student's attainment in mathematics. The purpose of the record is:

- to enable students to participate more effectively in determining the direction of their own learning
- to motivate students by making them more aware of their own progress
- to provide full diagnostic information for teachers which can serve as a basis for curriculum planning
- to provide information, summarised to whatever degree required for parents, employers, training schemes, further and higher education, head teachers, and so on.

THE STRUCTURE OF THE GAIM ASSESSMENT FRAMEWORK

The assessment has four inter-related components:

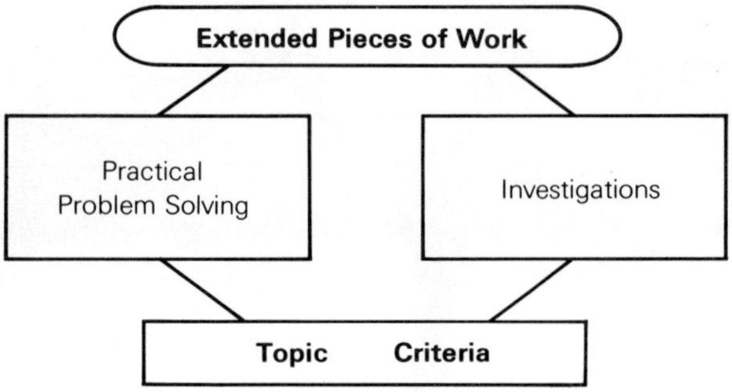

The practical problem solving and the investigations reflect the applied and the pure aspects of mathematics respectively. Each of these involves a variety of processes, some mathematical (e.g. estimating, transforming shapes) and some cross-curricular (e.g. talking, observing). The degree of success that they experience in each of these processes is critically dependent on the mathematical knowledge, understanding and skills a student has acquired. Within GAIM this knowledge, understanding and skill is expressed as topic criteria. These 'can do' statements are classified by level of difficulty and also by topic (Logic, Measurement, Number, Space, Statistics, Algebra/Functions). The structure of 15 levels of difficulty is being used in order to span the full range of achievement in 11–16-year-olds.

ASSESSING STUDENTS' WORK

Assessment is carried out by looking at the levels of achievement displayed by students in the four components: practical problem solving, investigations, extended pieces of work and topic criteria. The assessment is intended wherever possible to be integrated into the teaching scheme that the student is following. In order to assist teachers in using and assessing activities which are more open-ended, GAIM has devised some investigations and practical problems. In teachers' notes, level descriptions are suggested for each activity.

The open-ended activities are designed to encourage student decision-making and the integration of different skills. They are suitable for a wide attainment range and can be used with whole classes or with small groups of students or individuals. The student material for these activities is photocopiable and re-usable. The teachers' notes for each activity give all the necessary information about using the activity, such as the students for which the activity is suitable and the equipment needed.

INVESTIGATIONS involve students in mathematical explorations reflecting the pure aspects of mathematics. They are open-ended activities which provide students with the opportunity to develop their own systems for generating results and to identify and express the patterns they obtain.

Examples include:

- investigating the different symmetry patterns obtained by shading squares on a grid
- investigating the number of ways of giving change for different sums of money.

PRACTICAL PROBLEMS reflect the applied aspects of mathematics. There is no specified answer to each practical problem and students can produce a solution at a level of sophistication appropriate to their mathematical attainment.

Examples include:

- planning the layout of newspaper advertisements
- booking guests into appropriate rooms in a hotel
- finding out the ages and origins of local cars
- designing a wardrobe or bookcase.

Further details are available from GAIM Project, King's College, 552 King's Road, London SW10 0UA or from Macmillan Education, publishers of the GAIM Development Pack.

Oxford Certificate of Education Achievement (OCEA)

Over the last decade there has been growing support for the view that students can be encouraged to engage more actively in their own learning if that process is designed to help them assume a greater responsibility for it. At the same time attempts have been made to integrate assessment into the teaching and learning process in order to provide students with more frequent feedback on their learning and to provide the opportunity for the development of curricula more relevant to their needs.

OCEA has been developed by the University of Oxford Delegacy of Local Examinations in partnership with four LEAs (Coventry, Leicestershire, Oxfordshire and Somerset) and the University of Oxford Department of Educational Studies. Since September 1983 seconded teachers have been carrying out the research and development work on OCEA at the Delegacy.

OCEA looks at learning from three viewpoints which are expressed through its three components. The *P-component* provides a means whereby students can reflect on and record the whole range of their learning and development within and beyond the curriculum. The *G-component* recognises achievements within certain curriculum areas using specific criteria. The *E-component* provides a means whereby nationally/publicly recognised qualifications, and perhaps other school-based achievements, can be recorded.

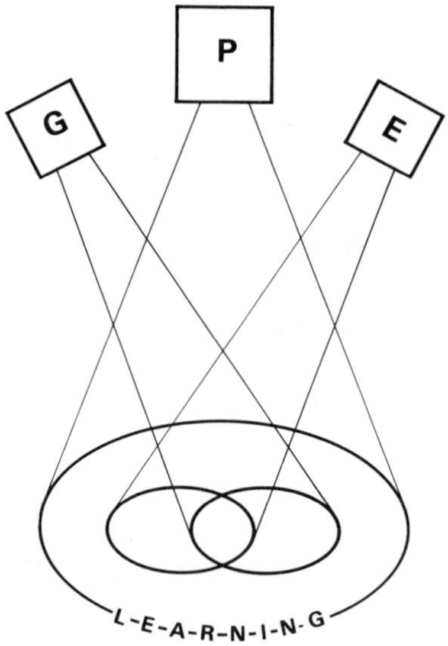

These three components are inter-dependent. This illustration shows how they focus upon the learning process, illuminating it from each of the viewpoints independently and from all three together.

MATHEMATICS WITHIN OCEA

Students will be encouraged to think and act mathematically rather than rote-learn a particular body of mathematical knowledge which may have a limited range of applications. The essential use of mathematics is to solve problems. *OCEA Mathematics* seeks to highlight the *processes* needed in problem solving. This involves the application of strategies, skills and reasoning, as described by the diagram below.

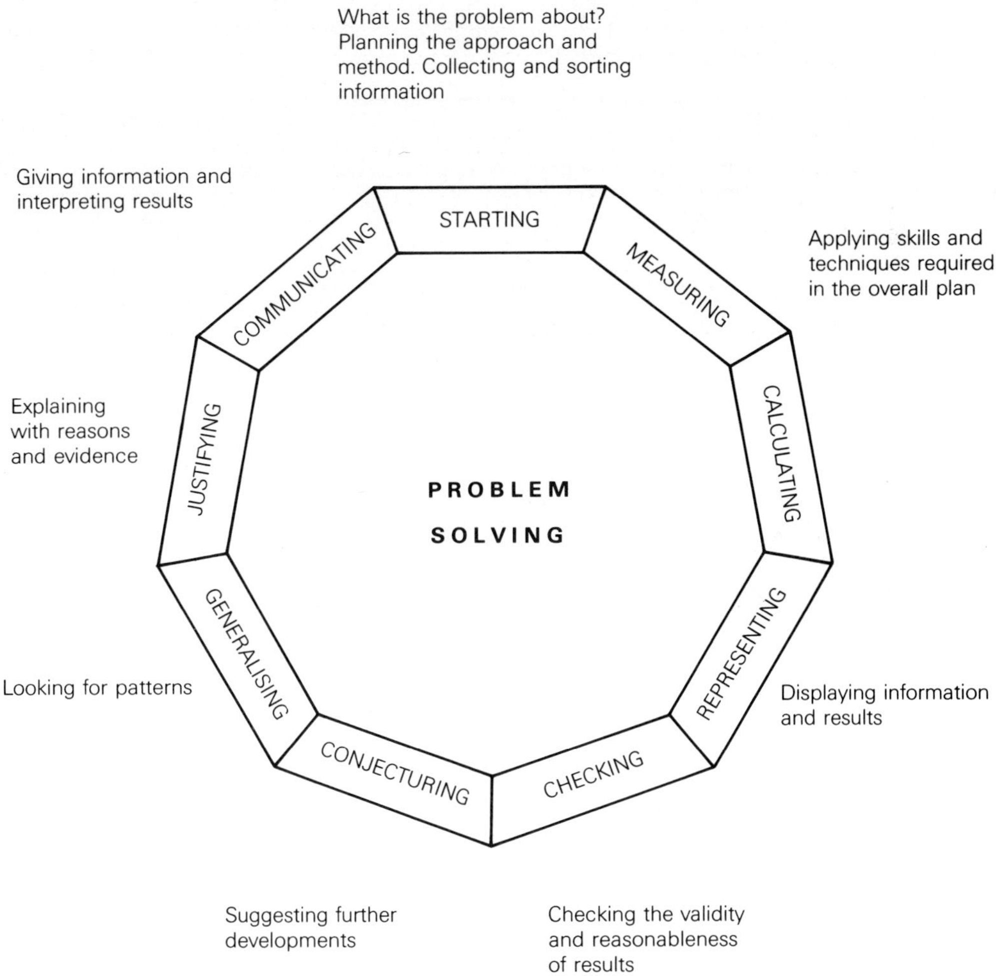

Further details are available from the University of Oxford Delegacy of Local Examinations, Ewart Place, Summertown, Oxford OX2 7BZ.

Appendix 2.4: A Summary o examining groups (*GCSE Coursework*

	S.E.G.	N.E.A.
% MARKS Course: Exam: Other:	40 50 Aural 14	25 75
PAPERS (All have three levels)	Sit 2 papers from a chain of 4. Level 1: Grades E - G Level 2: Grades C - F Level 3: Grades A - D Aural: 2 from a chain of 4.	Sit 2 papers from a chain of 4. Level P: Grades E - G Level Q: Grades C - F* Level R: Grades A - D* *Lower grades awarded in exceptional circumstances.
COURSEWORK ASSIGNMENTS	3 Units of work. One must be an 'extended piece'. Other two are 'single tasks' or a series of short assignments.	Centres are responsible for deciding nature of coursework. 'The length of a piece of work may vary from a few minutes activity to work pursue over several weeks.'
BOARD PRESCRIPTION AND GUIDANCE ON TASK CHOICE	'The provision of suitable activities is left to the teacher.' Together the units should involve all of the following selection: Data handling, problem solving, interpretations and generalisations of results, communication of results.	A list of possible activities is offered only as a guide. 'Teachers are free to devise their own assignments.'
ALLOCATION OF MARKS	Extended piece: 12 × 4 (weighting) 2 other units each: 12 × 2 (weighting) Oral aspect: 12 × 2 (weighting) Total: 120 scaled to 40	Practical work: 30 Investigation: 40 Assimilation: 30 Total: 100 scaled to 25
BOARD PRESCRIPTION AND GUIDANCE ON MARKING	4 pages of questions to ask either about the work or the pupil are offered as guidance. The teacher's aim is to award a grade first and numerical mark afterwards. Detailed cumulative grade descriptions are given.	Assessment guide outlines the main points a teacher should consider and the mark ranges which can be used. These include: Planning 0-12 Skills of using equipment 0- 6 Understanding of equipment 0-12 Clarity and conciseness of expression 0-10 Recall of knowledge 0- 3 Understanding of concepts and subject matter involved 0-10
MODERATION	Consortium consensus or by inspection by the board.	Statistically against written paper marks, but poor coursework cannot affect grades adversely (1988–1991).

CSE course work structures in the five
lathematics by Dr S. Pirie, Macmillan Educational)

1.E.G.	L.E.A.G.	W.J.E.C.
'5 5	25 70 Mental 5	22.2 74.1 Aural 3.7
different pairs of papers. 'oundation: Grades E - G ntermediate: C - F ligher: A - D	Sit 2 papers from a chain of 4. Level X: Grades E - G Level Y: Grades C - F Level Z: Grades A - D Mental: 3 different tests.	Sit 2 papers from a chain of 4. Level 1: Grades E - G Level 2: Grades C - F Level 3: Grades A - D Aural: 1 test for Levels 2 and 3, separate test for Level 1.
Assignments, each 2-3 weeks' 'ork. One from each of: ractical Geometry veryday Applications tatistics/Probability nvestigations :entre approved topic.	5 Investigations. One or two from each of: Pure Investigation Problems Practical work.	Level 1: An investigation of a particular theme using various mathematical techniques and three exercises demonstrating application of certain practical skills. Levels 2 and 3: A practical investigation and a problem solving investigation.
opics are suggested for each of ne task headings, but 'candidates re encouraged to select suitable opics outside this list.'	7 coursework tasks/investigations will be set by the board. Candidates may submit investigations of their own choice provided they fall into the required 3 categories.	A choice of 2 topics for each task at Levels 2 and 3 will be set. 2 topics and 4 exercises will be set for Level 1. Centres may choose their own topics provided they are of similar standard to those of the board.
or each task there are 4 marks or each of: esign/Strategy laths content ccuracy resentation and Clarity of rgument . Controlled Element (brief text r oral exchange) otal: 20 × 5 = 100 scaled to 5	Each task marked out of: 7 Strategy 7 Implementation and Reasoning 6 Interpretation and Communication Total: 20 × 5 = 100 scaled to 25	The marks are divided between: (i) The finished assignment. Understanding 3 Strategy 5 Content and Development 6 Communication 7 (ii) Continuous assessment including oral assessment. Understanding 3 Method 3 Conclusion 3 Total: 30 × 2 scaled to 22.2
he criteria for awarding 4, 2 nd 0 marks for each section of ach task are given.	The criteria for awarding 2, 5 and 7 marks for Strategy and Implementation and 1, 4 and 6 for Interpretation are given.	A description of the meaning of each of the headings is followed by the criteria for awarding each individual mark.
random sample by board's ssessors.	A random sample by board's Moderators.	Consortium moderation or by inspection by the board.

Appendix 3.1: Advice to Heads of Departments concerning Girls and Mathematics

An extract from *Girls and Mathematics* (Royal Society and IMA, 1986)

SECONDARY SCHOOL HEADS OF MATHEMATICS DEPARTMENTS

30. Research indicates that environmental pressures combine to conspire against girls achieving and participating as successfully as boys at mathematics. A particularly influential aspect of a pupil's environment is the school, and the way in which he or she relates to each subject is influenced by the environment in which it is taught. It is clear that mathematical skills are important for pupils in school when making subject option choices and later on in their lives and careers. Many pupils, in particular girls, underestimate the importance and use of mathematics. Girls are discouraged by the lack of role models around them that involve mathematics. Most heads of mathematics departments and others with positions of responsibility in schools are male. Girls and women are often absent completely from secondary school textbooks and teaching materials (including microcomputer software), examination questions are often sexist and marking schemes (in particular multiple choice papers) may disadvantage girls. Girls will respond better to mathematics if they work together in groups, are taught to be adventurous and not to be over-concerned with presentation ('the Tipp-Ex® syndrome'). Many of these problems can be overcome only by a proper awareness on the part of teachers. However, this will only be possible within a department that enables girls to reach their full potential in mathematics to the same degree as boys.

RECOMMENDATIONS TO SECONDARY SCHOOL HEADS OF MATHEMATICS DEPARTMENTS

31.

i) Initiate, support and actively encourage equal opportunity policies in the mathematics department and ensure that the teachers collectively identify the problem of the underparticipation and underachievement of girls in mathematics.

ii) As far as possible maintain a balance of men and women mathematics teachers. Girls taking A-levels in mathematics should be identified as role models to encourage girls lower down the school to continue with mathematics.

iii) Participate fully in careers counselling so that all pupils appreciate the value and importance of mathematics.

iv) Ensure that pupils appreciate the relevance of mathematics when making their option choices at age 13 or 14; liaise fully with other departments.

v) Encourage group work, discussion and a more adventurous teaching style to allow girls to develop fully their problem solving abilities.

vi) Ensure that teaching materials, especially textbooks, do not perpetuate sexist stereotypes; encourage staff to organise lively displays in the department depicting girls' mathematical work or girls using and enjoying mathematics.

vii) Where possible select non-sexist examination questions. Internal examinations should be balanced or neutral with respect to gender. Discourage multiple choice assessment.

viii) Ensure that girls and boys have equal and separate access to microcomputers when they are used in the mathematics classroom.

ix) As far as resources allow, ensure that the 6th form timetable is able to accommodate an A-level mathematics option with a broad range of A-level subject options.

x) Encourage women mathematics teachers to attend in-service training courses and to put themselves forward for promotion.

xi) Where pupils are divided into sets for mathematics, it may be preferable for the upper sets to be taught by women teachers in the early years of secondary school.

Appendix 4.1: Personal characteristics of managers in schools

Suggested check list for Head of Department

- Consult well before making decisions or implementing new ideas
- Provide opportunities for useful departmental discussion
- Take account of others' views when making a decision
- Be prepared to discuss and consider new ideas from colleagues
- Make positive decisions when required
- Communicate decisions well
- Inform the department of reasoning behind decisions

- Explain clearly departmental administrative procedures
- Keep colleagues informed as to what is going on in department
- Provide a clear scheme of work for each teaching group
- Provide adequate textbooks and other resources

- Delegate sufficiently
- Delegate appropriately
- Give necessary guidance and support when delegating

- Advise well on teaching or discipline when approached
- Take initiative in giving such advice
- Visit colleagues' lessons
- Encourage others to visit own lessons

- Be aware of colleagues' strengths and weaknesses
- Be aware of colleagues' interests and preferences
- Be aware of colleagues looking for extra responsibilities
- Be aware of colleagues who are under stress or other difficulties

- Bring out and foster colleagues' latent talent
- Inspire enthusiasm in colleagues
- Appreciate and praise colleagues' contributions

- Represent the department well in school management processes

CONSIDERATIONS RELATING TO THOSE WITH WHOM THEY WORK

- Consider the characteristics and practices of those to whom you are 'responsible' (e.g. Head, Deputy, Governors, Advisers, Parents). Which do you find helpful, encouraging, constructive, etc. and which do you find damaging, annoying, humiliating, difficult to handle, etc.? Do your answers suggest any ideas concerning your interaction with those who are responsible to you?
- Consider the characteristics and practices of those who are responsible to you. Classify them as above. Do these suggest any ideas concerning your interaction with those to whom you are responsible?

Appendix 4.2: Student teachers at Hartcliffe School

(An extract of notes for staff, students and training institutions)
The training of new teachers is an important function of any school. If we want good teachers we must be prepared to put time and effort into their training. Thus our guidelines for teaching practice are as follows:

STUDENTS SHOULD EXPECT FROM US

i) a timetable suiting the requirements of their course
ii) the opportunity to explore the pastoral role of teachers
iii) guidance in all aspects of teaching
iv) reasonable direction in the form of syllabuses, etc.
v) support in disciplinary matters
vi) an opportunity to see more of the school than just the faculty to which they are attached
vii) not to be used as gap-fillers for absent or busy staff, nor for register taking.

WE EXPECT FROM STUDENTS

i) the normal standards of dress and timekeeping expected of full members of staff
ii) that they should follow our procedure in the event of absence
iii) the setting of standards for the pupils similar to our own
iv) good record-keeping for continuity of classes
v) a willingness to participate in the life of the school, including attendance at year and faculty meetings.

THE SCHOOL AND STUDENTS

i) Students should have the opportunity during teaching practice to talk with:
   a) the Head
   b) a head of year
   c) faculty head(s) of subject(s) other than their own
   d) newly qualified teachers

ii) The opportunity should be provided for students to see examples of good teaching in their own and other subjects. This should be arranged informally through faculty heads for at least one period per week.
iii) Students should be encouraged to take part in clubs and other extra-curricular activities.

OUR HOPES

i) That students will enjoy teaching practice at Hartcliffe and find the experience useful and rewarding
ii) That we, and our pupils, will benefit from the enthusiasm and new ideas brought by student teachers
iii) That we will remember how exhausting teaching practice is; that we will recognise when our students are under pressure and try to relieve that pressure
iv) That students will bear in mind that giving them a useful experience represents a considerable extra workload for staff and that they will therefore forgive us the occasional hitch in their programme.

Appendix 4.3: Job specifications for mathematical posts

(Note that one job specification specifies the qualities desired, the other is explicit about the organisation of the department.)

BRIGHTON HILL SCHOOL
Teacher of Mathematics Scale 1

The Mathematics Department

The Mathematics Department consists of a team of six specialist teachers who are based in an extensive and attractive suite of purpose-built rooms which enjoys a very high level of provision. Mathematics forms part of a composite department comprising Mathematics, Business and Computer Studies.

A teacher is required to join this team which is highly active in the promotion of Mathematics throughout the school. The successful applicant will be expected to teach SMP Mathematics across a wide ability range.

The successful candidate will be required to:

i) Teach Mathematics to pupils throughout the school of widely differing ages and abilities
ii) Participate, as required, in the preparation of pupils for external examinations
iii) Within the wider context of the school, the successful candidate may be required to carry out with a positive commitment the role of a Group Tutor

The following attributes will be sought:

i) Liveliness, and imagination
ii) Enthusiasm, drive and initiative
iii) Perseverance and determination
iv) A genuine commitment to the subject, the department and the school, and a positive approach to all aspects of their work
v) Efficiency
vi) A willingness to take on responsibility
vii) Sound discipline both inside and outside the classroom and the ability to build sound relationships
viii) High personal standards and high expectations of others
ix) The ability to interest, inspire and motivate pupils

x) A genuine interest in pupils and a caring, sensitive attitude to them

xi) The ability to co-operate with and to relate well to other staff in the department. It is essential that the successful applicant should be able to work as a member of a team. This will involve willingness and ability to:

  a) motivate others, to bring new ideas into the department and to share them in a generous and unselfish way
  b) to support, advise and treat colleagues in a sensitive, tactful manner
  c) to compromise where necessary and to show commitment and enthusiasm for the ideas of others

xii) Willingness and enthusiasm to uphold the school's ethos and values

xiii) Ability to work co-operatively and supportively within the school structure

xiv) Good communication skills with colleagues and parents

xv) A neat and smart appearance

Hampshire County Council Policy Statement for all Scale 1 and Scale 2 posts:

Irrespective of his or her initial teaching programme the teacher may be asked to work with pupils in other age groups or to participate in alternative teaching approaches or subject areas.

Please note:
This information should be read in conjunction with the enclosed 'Notes for the Guidance of Applicants for Posts'.

April 1986

BRISLINGTON SCHOOL

The Mathematics Department

Mathematics is a compulsory subject throughout five years. The pupils are taught in mixed ability groups in Year 1; in Year 2 they spend part of their time in academic sets and part in mixed ability groups; in Years 3, 4 and 5 they are taught in academic sets. The basic text used throughout the five years is the SMP lettered series though other resources are available. In Years 1 and 2, when they are in mixed ability groups, they follow an individualised learning scheme based on the ideas of Nuffield Mathematics. In addition courses are offered at Sixth form level.

A wide range of external examinations are offered in the 4th and 5th Years;

LEAG - GCSE Mathematics Level Z (with coursework)
Level Y (with coursework)
Level X (with coursework)
GCSE Statistics Level Z (with coursework)

AEB - Foundation Level Mathematics (with coursework)

the aim being to tailor courses to pupils' needs.

In the 6th Form courses at present available are:

SUJB - A-level Mathematics
A-level Pure Mathematics and Statistics
A-level Pure Mathematics
A-level Applied Mathematics

As well as the Mathematics Department there is a Department for Special Education which operates throughout five years and which caters for children who are less able. They teach a variety of subjects to their pupils including Mathematics. There is also a small Support Unit for disturbed pupils.

There is a clear responsibility structure in the department carrying Incentive Allowances:

Head of Department	Incentive Allowance D
Assistant Head of Department	Incentive Allowance B
i/c Lower School Mathematics	Incentive Allowance A

and it is hoped to expand this in the future.

There is some specialist accommodation for Mathematics. The department is well-equipped and there is plenty of opportunity for an enthusiastic teacher to develop his/her ideas within the general framework laid down. Each teacher has a spread of age and ability on their timetable and one teacher will normally take a particular class for two years so as to give the pupils continuity of teaching. The department has three BBC micro-computers used for the teaching of Mathematics.

There is a separate Business and Information Technology Department offering a variety of examination and non-examination courses, including courses in Computer Education.

Conditions of Employment: This document is drawn up without prejudice to the Conditions of Employment which affects all teachers/heads. Interested candidates should regard this document as an opportunity to evaluate the expectations relating to the holder of this post.

Alan Rodgman, Head of Mathematics Department (April 1988)

Appendix 5.1: Section headings of a typical departmental handbook

i) Teaching schemes – philosophy of department
schemes for different pupil groups
book, page, exercise references
specimen questions

ii) Text books and other textual materials –
list of those in stock
storage systems
checking systems
replacement costs
procedure for lost books
procedure for issue and collection

iii) Pupil assessments – maintained year by year

iv) Set lists, current timetable

v) Resources available – stationery, films, models, computer availability, software catalogue with comments, local teachers' centre

vi) Homework policy

vii) Procedures with exceptional pupils, including very high and low abilities

viii) Disciplinary procedures

ix) Reports and communication with parents

x) Internal assessment procedures

xi) Policy and regulations for external exams

xii) Calculator policy

xiii) Staff absence procedure

xiv) Details of main feeder schools

xv) Procedures for exceptional times of the year, e.g. end of term

Appendix 5.2: Considering a new textbook

i) Define philosophy and objectives of course in question; is a textbook likely to be a useful resource? If so . . .

ii) Assess requirements with staff involved:

- topic content
- depth of treatment
- explanations, compatability with teacher
- worked examples
- exercises, degree of difficulty, grading

iii) Search publishers' catalogues, bookshops, teachers' centre library

iv) Seek experience of other schools, adviser etc.

v) Send off for inspection copies

vi) Circulate inspection copies to staff with list of criteria for assessment, for example:

- headings under ii) above
- look of book, attractiveness, heaviness
- usefulness of illustrations
- suitability of notation
- relevance of examples to real situations
- implications for classroom management
- durability
- value for money
- other resources required

vii) Staff meeting to discuss and decide

viii) Order one set of chosen book and put into immediate use

ix) Send back or buy other inspection copies

x) Assess chosen book in light of experience before making final decision

xi) It is very unlikely that any book will perfectly fit the bill, hence . . . prepare and circulate notes on the use of the book emphasising particularly useful sections and drawing attention to areas where supplementary material may be necessary.

Appendix 5.3: Departmental responsibilities

MATHEMATICS DEPARTMENT DIARY 1986/7
OUT OF TIMETABLE ACTIVITIES

Junior Maths Club	Thursdays 1.40 p.m.	DSB
Junior Maths Puzzles	Fortnightly	GPS
Junior Maths Quiz	Thursdays; Feb/Mar	AJP
Junior Maths Mag.	One per term	DSB/GPS
Lent Sponsored Maths	March	ALS
Senior Maths Society	C. 2 meetings/term	AJP
Senior Maths Puzzles	C. 4 per term	RML
Hans Woyda Contest	Autumn/Spring	ALS
National Maths Contest	February/March	GPS
Gnomon	1/2 per year	RML
Field Day, 4th form	September	DSB
Field Day, 1st form	September	GPS/JCH/PJR
Field Day, 1st form	May	GPS/DSB/MFW

CHORES

Maths Dpt. Library	DSB
Small items apparatus, visual aids, grid papers etc.	JCH
Practical Mechanics	JCH
Practical Statistics	AJP
Videos	GPS
Stock of JOCSE/GCSE paper & solutions	ALS
Stock of 'A' level Maths papers/solns (London, MEI)	AJP
Stock of Further Maths papers/solns	AJP
Stock of Further Maths papers/solns	RML

INTERNAL SYLLABUS AND EXAMS

YEAR GROUP	YEAR MANAGER	DEC/JAN/FEB EXAM	SUMMER EXAM
Junior	DSB	DSB	IAG
First	DSB	individual	AWA
Second	RML	individual	KAC/AJP
Third	PJR/AJP	individual	PJR/DSB
Fourth	GPS	individual	GPS: Paper 1 for all JCH: Paper 2 for M3, 4, 5 ALS: Papers 2 for M1, 2
Fifth	—	ALS: P1 for all	—

(Trinity School, Croydon.)

Appendix 5.4: Internal examinations

General

i) Maintain data-base of test papers/items emending and developing each year.

ii) Centralise storage of papers and mark schemes for security.

iii) Post exam comments on items, to be collected and stored, ready for following year and curriculum review.

iv) Post exam comments on teaching groups to be appended to list of results.

Procedure

v) List of results in rank/alphabetical/form order.

vi) Indicate with ↑ or ↓ significant differences from normal/expected progress of pupil.

vii) Append comments to list reporting progress of group.

viii) A separate exam report indicating the effectiveness of individual test items.

ix) Comments on teaching difficulties of particular topics.

Interpretation

x) Assemble information to compare performance in different groups. This will enable some check of setting accuracy/teacher success.

xi) Consider comments on effectiveness of test items in light of (x), then produce revision guide for next year's test.

xii) Consider comments on teaching difficulties with possibility of curriculum amendment.

Appendix 6.1: Preliminary checklist of mathematics inquiries from the Science Department

From notes relating to liaison between science and maths departments (March 1982).

Science department topic inquiry	Mathematics department comment
Bar charts, all first-year forms, September	May of first year
Area, all first-year forms, September	March of first year
Measure 100 sheets paper and divide by 100	Yes
$3.7 = \frac{10.1}{R}$ second year. 'A' band, October	End of third year
$\frac{1}{u} = \frac{1}{v} - \frac{1}{f}$ Also solve for v, f, second year. 'A' band February	End of third year
Proportionality, dependent and independent variables. Third year. 'A' band mid year	Mid third year
Gradient – linear function. Third year mid year	Mid third year
Sine as an angular measure. Third year September	End second year, early third
Decimals correct to one, two places. All first-year forms, mid year	No first-year forms
Long division, integers. All forms second year November	Yes
Long division decimal values for 'A' and 'B' bands	In 'A' band, yes
Measuring to 1% accuracy – choice of instrument – decimal places in result. 'A' band in third year	Yes
$(a + b)^2$ and $(a + b)^3$ in third years. 'A' band	Neither at all
Routine use of logs. Second year. 'A' band and other bands third year	Yes
Estimating prior to slide rule or calculator. Second year all forms	Yes
Adequate practice in long division in third year scheme	Reply awaited

Appendix 6.2: Council for the Accreditation of Teacher Education

Criteria for the accreditation of courses of initial teacher training

The following is a digest of the criteria which the Council is expected to apply after considering its advice to the Secretaries of State for Education and Science, and for Wales regarding individual courses for initial teacher training.

Certain of these criteria were laid down originally in DES Circular 3/84 (Welsh Office Circular 21/84). They were supplemented in October 1984 in the light of advice which had been given to the Secretaries of State by the Advisory Committee on the Supply and Education of Teachers, on the training of secondary school teachers in the teaching of second subjects. These additional criteria were announced in Teacher Training Circular Letter 7/84.

The digest has been prepared in this form as an aid to those involved in the planning, organisation and running of initial teacher training courses, and those concerned to assess how far individual courses meet the criteria. It is not a definite restatement of the criteria themselves, but should be used in conjunction with the original statements of the criteria.

It will be noted that not all of the criteria apply to all types of courses.

SELECTION OF STUDENTS

i) Institutions should have adequate procedures for assessing whether candidates show the personal and intellectual qualities suitable for teaching, and evidence of professional potential.

ii) The procedures should involve a personal or group interview with each candidate, and at some stage should involve experienced practising schoolteachers.

iii) The procedures should provide equal opportunities at all stages for all candidates, regardless of race or sex.

iv) In assessing personal qualities institutions should look in particular for a sense of responsibility; a robust but balanced outlook; awareness; sensitivity; enthusiasm; and a facility for effective communication in spoken and written English and, where appropriate, Welsh.

v) Previous employment or self-employment, or experience of work with children or adolescents in a school, youth club or otherwise, should normally count in a candidate's favour.

vi) All entrants should have attained in mathematics and in English the standard required for Grade C or above in GCE or Grade 1 in CSE.
vii) All entrants should have a satisfactory health record.
viii) Entrants to *undergraduate* courses should fulfil normal academic requirements for admission to first degree studies, or be mature entrants with acceptable alternative qualifications.
ix) Such alternative qualifications should include suitable personal qualities; relevant experience of adult and working life; the intellectual capacity to complete a degree course successfully; and competence in the understanding and use of mathematics and English. Both the institution and the validating body should be satisfied of the adequacy of these qualifications.
x) The standards of courses, and of end-of-course qualifications awarded, should not be compromised in order to accommodate such students. They should not exceed 25 per cent of the intake to any one course.
xi) Undergraduate students intending to teach *primary* pupils should have a broad base of studies at GCE O- and A-levels.
xii) Those intending to teach *secondary* pupils should normally hold an A-level pass, or equivalent, appropriate to their main and second teaching subjects.
xiii) Entrants to *postgraduate* courses should hold a degree of a UK university or the CNAA, or a recognised equivalent qualification.
xiv) The degree should be suitably related to the work of primary or secondary schools, as appropriate.
xv) In determining acceptance for second subject method training in a postgraduate course, favourable consideration should be given to students who have studied the subject, or a related one, in their first degree course.

STAFF

i) Staff should be equipped to educate and train entrants to an all-graduate profession, and to prepare undergraduate students in their main and second subjects at a level appropriate to higher education.
ii) Staff concerned with pedagogy should have had recent successful experience as teachers of the age range for which they are preparing students, and should maintain regular and frequent experience of classroom teaching.
iii) For those unable to meet this requirement there should be opportunities to demonstrate their teaching effectiveness in schools.

COURSE ORGANISATION

i) All courses should have the support of a local committee representing the institution, LEAs in the area, practising teachers, and members of the community outside the education service. This committee should meet regularly, discuss the planning, operation and review of the courses, and promote links between the institution, schools and the community.
ii) Courses should be developed and run in close working partnership with a number and variety of schools.

iii) Experienced teachers should be involved in the planning, supervision, support and assessment of students' practical work in schools, and in their training within the institution.
iv) Postgraduate courses should be of not less than 36 weeks' duration.

SUBJECT STUDIES AND SUBJECT METHOD

i) The higher education and initial teacher training of students should include the equivalent of at least two full years course time devoted to subject studies at a level appropriate to higher education.
ii) In undergraduate courses for primary teachers, the specialism may cover a wide area of the curriculum, and the time allocated to it should include the application of the subjects concerned to the learning and developmental needs of young children.
iii) In undergraduate courses for secondary teachers, the two years should be spent in the study of not more than two subjects from within the present or developing secondary school curriculum.
iv) Adequate attention should be given to the methodology of teaching the subjects chosen, and relating them to the curriculum as a whole and to the everyday life and work of the community.
v) Intending primary teachers should also devote at least 100 hours, through a combination of taught time, school experience and private study, to studying the teaching of language, and its significance across the curriculum. Similar time should also be devoted to mathematics.
vi) The study and teaching practice of intending primary teachers, especially those intending to teach children in the early years, should embrace all relevant areas of the curriculum including religious education.
vii) Where secondary courses provide substantial preparation for the teaching of a second subject, the time and attention given to it should amount to at least one third of that given to the methodology of teaching the main subject.
viii) In an undergraduate course for secondary teachers, the academic study of a main and a second subject should be similarly apportioned.

EDUCATIONAL AND PROFESSIONAL STUDIES

i) Courses of up to three years should provide at least 15 weeks of school experience and teaching practice. Four year courses should provide at least 20 weeks.
ii) Educational and professional studies and practical school experience should all be closely linked.
iii) Practical school experience should include both intermittent and block practice; should provide for observation, for small group teaching, and for the tutoring of individuals; and should offer responsibility for organising and planning the work of a whole class and experience of class management and control.
iv) Teaching method should differentiate according to the student's intended age group.
v) Students should experience a wide range of teaching and learning methods and be given ample opportunity to discuss and assess them.

vi) Students should experience and understand the contribution of new technologies to all aspects of children's learning.

vii) Students should be given an adequate mastery of basic professional skills. The course elements leading to this need not be formally integrated into the course's structure, but should be designed, through the structuring of school experience and through institution-based teaching and study, to achieve this purpose.

viii) Students should be prepared for the diversity of ability, behaviour, social background and ethnic and cultural origins encountered in ordinary schools; and in how to respond to that diversity and guard against preconceptions based on race or sex.

ix) Students should be prepared to recognise, understand and cope with different levels of performance, including special needs and gifts.

x) Students should be prepared for the pastoral and administrative responsibilities of teaching, and aware of the teacher's relationships with colleagues, parents and the community.

xi) Students should acquire an appreciation of the structure and administration of the education service and be able to see their role as a teacher within the broader context of educational purposes.

xii) Students should understand the nature, values and economic foundations of contemporary society and the relationship between the school curriculum and the adult world.

STUDENT ASSESSMENT AND CERTIFICATION

i) Qualifications carrying qualified teacher status should never be awarded to students whose practical classroom work is satisfactory.

ii) The professional teaching performance of undergraduates should be judged separately from their academic performance.

iii) There should be arrangements for the early identification, and transfer to other courses, of students who are satisfactory academically but unsuited to teaching.

Council for the Accreditation of Teacher Education, Elizabeth House, York Road, London SE1 (January, 1985).

Appendix 7: Sources and resources

Books

Clearly no list can be comprehensive but the listing which follows aims to provide further reading on many of the themes developed in this book.

HEAD OF DEPARTMENT ROLE

M. Marland, *Head of Department* (Heinemann, 1971).

M. Marland and S. Hill, *Departmental Management* (Heinemann, 1982).

Hertfordshire County Council, *A Professional Handbook for Heads of Mathematics Departments* (Hertfordshire County Council, 1981).

Mathematical Association. The Board of the Diploma in the Management of Mathematics Departments in Secondary Schools. Papers arising from a Conference (1986).

D. John, *Leadership in Schools* (Heinemann, 1980).

R. G. Bloomer, 'The Role of Head of Department: Some Questions and Answers', *Educational Research*, 22(2), (1980).

J. C. Hall, and J. B. Thomas, 'Mathematics Department Headship in Secondary Schools - Research Report', *Educational Administration*, 5(2), 30–7 (1977).

J. Howson and B. Woolhough, 'Head of Department - Dictator or Democrat?' *Educational Management and Administration*, 10, 37–43 (1982).

The Association for Science Education, *Help for New Heads of Science* (ASE, 1987).

British Gas/Association for Science Education, *Management in School Science Departments* (4 units)

- Understanding Managerial Roles
- Meetings as Vehicles of Communication
- Staff Development - Selection and Appraisal
- Time Management (British Gas/ASE, 1981).

Mathematical Association, *Starting as a Mathematics Teacher* (MA, 1986).

K. Selkirk, *Teaching Mathematics* (Macmillan, 1984).

H. Shuard and D. Quadling, *Teachers of Mathematics* (Harper & Row, 1980).

E. C. Wragg, *Teacher Appraisal* (Macmillan, 1987).

THE MATHEMATICS CURRICULUM

C. Bentley and D. Malvern, *Guides to Assessment in Education: Mathematics* (Macmillan, 1983).

Committee of Inquiry into the Teaching of Mathematics in Schools (Cockcroft Report), *Mathematics Counts* (HMSO, 1982).

A. Craft and G. Klein, *Agenda for Multicultural Teaching*, Ch. 18, 64–6 (Longman, 1986).

DES, *Mathematics from 5 to 16*, HMI Curriculum Matters Series, No. 3 (HMSO, 1985).

DES, *GCSE The National Criteria – Mathematics* (DES, 1985).

A. G. Howson, 'Curriculum Development & Curriculum Research', Part C of *A Review of Research in Mathematical Education* (NFER-Nelson, 1983).

ICMI, *School Mathematics in the 1990s* (Cambridge University Press, 1986).

Mathematical Association, *Why, What and How?* (MA, 1976).

Schools Council, *The Mathematical Curriculum: A Critical Review*, several volumes including Geometry, Mathematics Across the Curriculum (Blackie/Chambers, 1977).

H. Shuard, *Primary Mathematics Today and Tomorrow* (Longman, 1986).

L. Stenhouse, *An Introduction to Curriculum Research & Development* (Heinemann, 1975).

D. Woodrow 'Multicultural Issues' in *Times Educational Supplement*, 11 May (Times Publishing, 1984).

TEACHING AND LEARNING MATHEMATICS

A. W. Bell, J. Costello and D. Küchemann, 'Research on Learning and Teaching', Part A of *A Review of Research in Mathematical Education* (NFER-Nelson, 1983).

T. H. F. Brissenden, *Mathematics Teaching* (Harper & Row, 1980).

M. Cornelius, *Teaching Mathematics* (Croom Helm, 1982).

P. Dean, *Teaching and Learning Mathematics* (Woburn, 1982).

L. Dickinson, M. Brown and O. Gibson, *Children Learning Mathematics* (Holt Educational, 1984).

A. Floyd, *Developing Mathematical Thinking* (OU, 1981).

K. Hart (ed.), *Children's Understanding of Mathematics 11–16* (Murray, 1981).

R. Harvey, D. Kerslake, H. Shuard and M. Torbe, *Language, Learning and Teaching 6: Mathematics* (Ward Lock, 1985).

Z. Isaacson, *Teaching GCSE Mathematics* (Hodder & Stoughton, 1987).

A. Orton, *Learning Mathematics* (Cassell, 1987).

School Mathematics Project, *Watch Your Language*, INSET pack (SMP, 1985).

H. Shuard and A. Rothery (ed.), *Children Reading Mathematics* (Murray, 1984).

PUPILS WITH PARTICULAR NEEDS

A. Ahmed *et al.*, *Mathematics for Low Attainers* (West Sussex Institute, 1985).

B. Denver, C. Stolz and M. Brown, *Low Attainers in Mathematics 5 to 16* (Methuen, 1982).

Low Attainers in Mathematics Project (LAMP), *Better Mathematics* (HMSO, 1987).

Mathematical Association, *Working Mathematically with Low Attainers* Videotape (MA/OU, 1986).

Mathematical Association in conjunction with NARE, *Struggle,* Magazine for teachers working with low attainers, (MA, Termly).

Mathematical Association, Booklist - *Pupils with special needs* (MA, Regularly updated).

Mathematical Association, *Plus*, Magazine for more able secondary pupils (MA, Termly).

Mathematical Association, Booklist - *Books for use with gifted children* (MA, Regularly updated).

Royal Society & Institute of Mathematics and its Applications, *Girls and Mathematics* (Royal Society, 1986).

A. Straker, *Mathematics for Gifted Pupils* (Longman, 1983).

The Open University in association with ILEA, *Girls into Mathematics* (Cambridge University Press, 1986).

Inner London Education Authority, *Everyone Counts* (ILEA, 1985).

BEYOND THE DEPARTMENT

A. Fitzgerald, *Mathematics in Employment (16–18)* (University of Bath, 1981).

A. Fitzgerald, *New Technology and Mathematics in Employment* (University of Birmingham, 1985).

J. F. Ling, *Mathematics Across the Curriculum* (Blackie, 1978).

Mathematical Association, *Interface*, Links between primary and secondary schools (MA, 1983).

Mathematical Association, *Sharing Mathematics with Parents* (MA, 1987).

Royal Society, *Mathematics - Physics Interface in Schools* (Royal Society, 1986).

School Mathematics Project, *Communicating with Parents*, INSET pack (SMP, 1984).

Secondary Examinations Council and Open University, *GCSE Guide for Teachers* (OU, 1986).

M. Smith and G. Taylor, *How to Type Mathematics and Science* (Stanley Thornes, 1984).

A. D. Turner, K. Hart and L. Booth, 'Collaboration between mathematics and science departments' in *Mathematics in School* (4 issues) (Longman, 1982).

REFERENCES TO FURTHER SOURCES

Centre for Studies in Science and Mathematics Education:

- *References of Use to Teachers of Mathematics* (University of Leeds, 1974).
- *Supplement 1* (University of Leeds, 1979).
- *Supplement 2* (University of Leeds, 1987).

(Provide references to articles in some eighteen mathematics and mathematics education journals since 1961.)

Association of Teachers of Mathematics, *Materials for Mathematics* (ATM, 1984). (Listing of materials and details of suppliers.)

F. R. Watson, *Ideas in the Teaching of Mathematics and Science (ITeMS)*, Issue v. (University of Keele, 1987).
(A frequently updated catalogue of materials published by colleges, universities, resource centres and individuals.)

Journals

FOR TEACHERS

Mathematics in School	(Concerned with school mathematics, 7–16 years.) Five issues per year. Available direct from Longman or through membership of the Mathematical Association.
Mathematical Gazette	(Mainly secondary and beyond.) Published by the Mathematical Association. Four issues per year through membership of the Association.
Mathematics Teaching	(Primary and secondary.) Published by the Association of Teachers of Mathematics. Four issues per year, through membership of ATM.
Micromath	A journal of ATM exploring the potential of the computer for creating mathematical activity obtainable through membership of ATM or from Basil Blackwell Ltd.
Struggle	Mathematics for Low Attainers. Originally produced by the Inner London Education Authority, this is now being distributed by The Mathematical Association.
Teaching Statistics	(For teachers of pupils 9–19.) Three issues per year. Obtainable from the Department of Probability and Statistics, University of Sheffield S10 2TN.
Teaching Mathematics and Its Applications	Published by the Institute of Mathematics and its Applications. Three issues per year.

Investigator — A newspaper style magazine to encourage problem solving and investigational work in the classroom. SMILE, Middle Row School, Kensal Road, London W10. Three issues per year.

Times Educational Supplement — Normally two special 'Mathematics' supplements each year.

MATHEMATICS MAGAZINES FOR SECONDARY PUPILS

(in roughly ascending order of mathematical sophistication).

Factor — SMILE (ILEA), Middle Row School, Kensal Road, London W10 (£3.50 for ten).

Number — Resources for Learning Unit, Bishop Road, Bristol BS7 8LS. Three issues per year (£1.50 for ten).

Mathematical Pie — Available from Mathematical Association (from 26p to 13p each depending on quantity).

Plus — Mathematical Association. Once per term (60p).

Hypotenuse — Mathematical Journal for Secondary School students. Dr. Judita Cofman, 16 Cranford Lodge, 80 Victoria Drive, London SW19 6HH (£3.00 annual subscription for three issues).

Mathematical Spectrum — Applied Probability Trust, Hicks Building, The University, Sheffield S3 7RH (£4.00 for three issues).

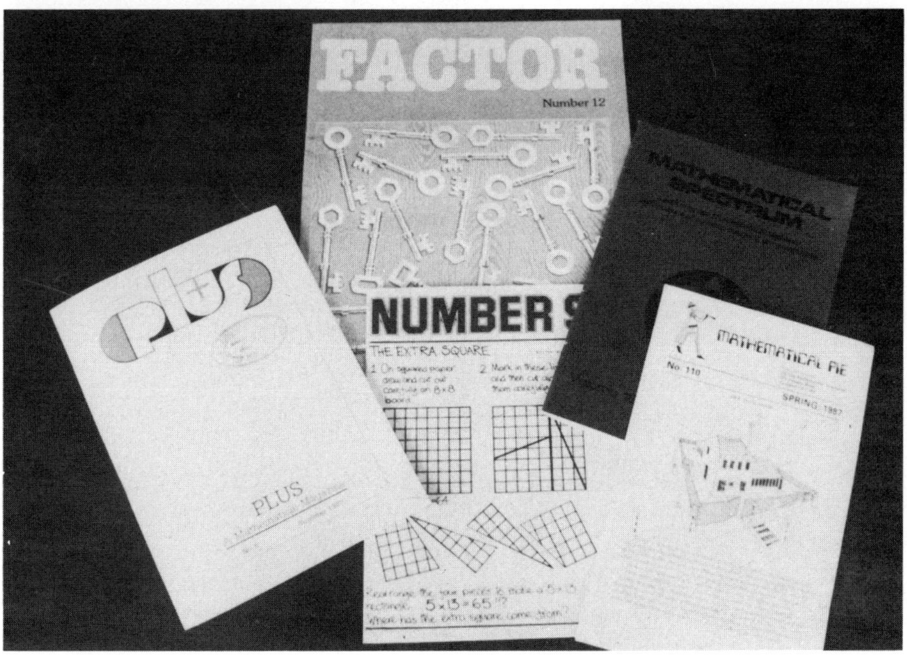

Materials for mathematics teaching

Mathematics Teaching and *Mathematics in School* frequently carry reports and reviews of new apparatus and games. So also does the *Times Educational Supplement*. The ATM leaflet *Materials for Mathematics* carries an extensive list with addresses of suppliers.

Catalogues of equipment and stationery are available from:

E. J. Arnold, Parkside Lane, Leeds LS11 5TD. (0532 772112)

Creative Publications, 3977 East Bayshore Road, PO Box 10328, Palo Alto, California 94303, USA.

Hestair Hope Ltd., St Philips Drive, Royton, Oldham OL2 6AG. (061-652 1411)

Cuisenaire Company Limited, 11 Crown Street, Reading, Berkshire. (0734 873101)

Excitement in Learning (Copyprints), 88 Mint Street, London SE1. (01-407 2079)

Inner London Education Authority, Centre for Learning Resources, 275 Kennington Lane, London SE11 5QZ.

Invicta Plastics Ltd., Education Aids Division, Oadby, Leics. (0533 717211)

Philip and Tacey Ltd., Northway, Andover, Hants SP10 5BA. (0264 61171)

Taskmaster Ltd., Morris Road, Leicester LE2 6BR. (0533 704286)

Tarquin Publications, Stradbroke, Diss, Norfolk IP21 5JP. (037 984218) Listings include DIME and Leapfrogs materials.

Also as listed in F. R. Watson's ITeMS. (See Books - References to further sources.)

Posters

Producers of wall charts and posters include:

BP Educational Service, PO Box 21, Redhill, Surrey.

Creative Publications, PO Box 10328, Palo Alto, Calif. 94303, USA.

SMILE, Middle Row School, Kendal Road, London W10.

The Mathematical Association, 259 London Road, Leicester LE2 3BE.

Pictorial Charts Educational Trust, 27 Kirchen Road, London W13 0UD.

Tarquin Publications, Stradbroke, Diss, Norfolk IP21 5JP.

Audio-visual material

Video tape is rapidly becoming the most available and flexible medium for audio-visual presentation. However, although it is relatively easy to record schools broadcasts, 'off air', it can be much more difficult to create copies of 'classics' of the past and new privately made presentations.

FILM CATALOGUES

Two extensive listings of mathematical films are:

Association of Teachers of Mathematics, List of Mathematical Films and Film Loops, £1.15 (1976).

Singmaster, D. (compiler) List of 16 mm Films on Mathematical subjects, Faculty of Mathematics, Open University, Milton Keynes MK7 6AA £1.00 (1979).

Both catalogues contain names and addresses of distributors (some 'films' are now available in video format from Edward Patterson Associates, Treetops, Cannongate Road, Hythe, Kent CT21 2PT). Reviews of new films and accounts of their use in the classroom appear in *Mathematics Teaching*.

FREE LOAN

Most films are not cheap to hire but you may find that one or more of the following local sources have small film libraries which can be used by local schools:

The LEA Mathematics Adviser
The Teachers' Centre
College, Polytechnic or University Department of Education

Several commercial companies also make films available for a minimal charge but understandably the subjects may not be entirely relevant:

ICL, Computer House, 322 Euston Road, London NW1 3BD.
IBM Film Library, 25 The Burroughs, Hendon, London NW4 4AD.
The BP Film Library, 15 Beaconsfield Road, London NW10 2LE. (01-451 1129)

PRODUCERS AND DISTRIBUTORS OF FILMSTRIPS AND SLIDES

Visual Publications, 197 Kensington High Street, London W8 6BB. (01-937 1568)

The Slide Centre Ltd., 143 Chatham Road, London SW11 5BR. (01-223 3457)

Prismatron Productions Ltd., 9 Gloucester Crescent, London NW1 7DS. (01-485 3582)

Tarquin Publications, Stradbroke, Diss, Norfolk IP21 5JP. (037 984218)

TELEVISION AND RADIO

BBC & ITV Schools Broadcasts, (BBC School Publications, 35 Marylebone High Street, London W1M 4AA and ITV Publications, 247 Tottenham Court Road, London W1).

Open University Programmes in Mathematics and Mathematical Education. (The Open University, Milton Keynes, Bucks MK7 6AA.)

VIDEO RECORDINGS FOR INSET

ILEA: Organisation and Classroom Management
Mathematics in the Classroom (three units relating to investigations and problem solving).

Open University: Working Mathematically with Low Attainers (with MA)
Secondary Mathematics: Classroom Practice.

Shell Centre, University of Nottingham: Teaching with a Micro.

Organisations involved in mathematics education

Association of Teachers of Mathematics, 7 Shaftesbury Street, Derby DE3 8YB. (0332 46599)

Founded in 1952. Publications include the journal *Mathematics Teaching*, *Micromath*, occasional books and a variety of development material by local groups. Local group meetings and annual conference at Easter. Subscription (1987) £22.00 per annum. Student subscription £11.00 per annum.

Department of Education and Science, Elizabeth House, 39 York Road, London SE1 7PH.

The DES has not been directly concerned with the curriculum in schools, but during the eighties has become increasingly influential through reports and by requiring LEAs to be more explicit regarding the curriculum in the schools. Its future role in relation to the National Curriculum is not yet clear. It has funded many post-Cockcroft initiatives involving curriculum, assessment and in-service training.

Her Majesty's Inspectors are concerned with the curriculum areas and a number have particular responsibilities in mathematics teaching. Occasional papers, some of a general nature, some directly relevant to the teaching of mathematics, are published by both DES and HMI. HMI also run a number of in-service courses throughout the country.

Institute of Mathematics and its Applications, Maitland House, Warrior Square, Southend-on-Sea, Essex SS1 2JY.

The professional institution to which mathematicians can belong. There are various grades of membership corresponding to the professional qualifications of the members. The institute organises conferences on a number of topics of mathematical concern, especially on applications in industry and in society.

The Institute's publications include a journal for research papers, a bulletin for expository articles and current news, and occasional publications on careers, qualifications and courses in mathematics.

Joint Mathematical Council

The JMC consists of nominated representatives of most other mathematical organisations. It is a committee at which information is exchanged, and where the efforts of the constituent organisations can be co-ordinated.

Under the aegis of the JMC, certain funds from industry have been dispensed to provide schoolmaster fellowships and in-service training schemes.

Scottish Mathematical Council

The Council has representatives of universities, colleges, the Scottish Education Department, the Regional Education Authorities, schools, commerce and industry. They organise project competitions, an annual mathematical challenge, masterclasses and conferences. An annual newsletter is published (Secretary: C. J. Wood, Heriot Watt University, Riccarton, Edinburgh EH14 4AS (031-449 5111 Ext. 2360.)

The Mathematical Association, 259 London Road, Leicester LE2 3BE (0533 703877).

Founded in 1871. Over the years the MA has produced a series of influential reports on the teaching of mathematics. Publications include the *Mathematical Gazette*, dealing with comparatively advanced levels of teaching and minor research, and containing an unsurpassed collection of reviews; *Mathematics in School*, covering mathematics teaching up to the age of 16; occasional publications. Local group meetings and annual Easter conference. Annual subscription (1988) £31.00 (all journals and reports). Reduced subscription (1988) £12.00 for students and those under 25.

Mathematical Olympiads

Annual competitions are held under the auspices of the National Committee for Mathematical Contests, a committee of the Mathematical Association, from which detailed information and past papers are available (see above).

i) National Mathematics Contest (Autumn). A multiple-choice test usually taken by about 12 000 boys and girls in the United Kingdom.

ii) About 200 competitors selected after good performances on the NMC participate in the British Mathematical Olympiad (April).

iii) Further International Selection Test (FIST) (May). The BMO has got the same syllabus and format as the International Mathematical Olympiad. From good performance on BMO a few (20–45) are invited to take FIST. From performances on (ii), (iii) and during a training and selection weekend and comments from their teachers the team for the International Mathematical Olympiad is selected. Teams usually consist of six pupils and the IMO takes place in July in the country of one of the competing teams. In 1985, 38 countries entered teams.

Royal Society, 6 Carlton House Terrace, London SW1Y 5AG.

The premier scientific society of the world; election to the Royal Society is a high academic honour. The Royal Society is concerned with education in a number of ways. One of its committees, the British National Committee for Mathematics is the link with international organisations such as the International Committee for Mathematical Instruction, which arranges a world-wide conference on mathematical education every four years.

School Mathematics Project (SMP), The Executive Officer SMP, University of Southampton SU9 5NH.

An independent educational trust, which has published various textbooks and teaching materials for the age range 7–18 over the last 20 years. The commercial success of the Project's materials has enabled it to fund further developmental work on a substantial scale. A news-sheet is published twice each year.

Standing Committee of Associations concerned with Mathematics Education in Schools – SCAMES. Secretary: Mr W Brookes, Department of Education, University of Southampton.

This group was formed to bring together representatives of ATM, MA, NAMA (National Association of Mathematics Advisers), AUMET (Association of University Mathematics Education Teachers) and the mathematics section of NATFHE (National Association of Teachers in Further and Higher Education). It responds to major developments in mathematics education in schools and aims to give a lead in future development.

Appendix 8: An invitation to join the Mathematical Association

The Mathematical Association is for you if you teach mathematics at any age or stage from 4 years onwards. You do not need to be a high-powered mathematician to belong to the Association. One of its strengths is that it brings together primary, secondary and university teachers, industrialists and advisers.

Benefits of membership

JOURNALS AND PUBLICATIONS

According to the subscription paid members receive one or more of the following journals:

i) The *Mathematical Gazette* is published four times a year. It offers articles on current issues in mathematical teaching at all levels of secondary school, college and university. It includes full book reviews.

ii) *Mathematics in School* is published five times a year covering the teaching of the 7–16 age range. It is a lively, brightly coloured magazine, closely related to the classroom.

iii) *Mathematics round the Country* is of particular interest to primary teachers and is obtainable directly from the Association or, at a reduced rate for quantity, through your local education authority

iv) *Struggle*, published jointly with the National Association for Remedial Education, three times a year, is concerned with the teaching of low attainers.

REPORTS

Members receive, at no extra charge, a copy of new reports produced by Teaching Committee.

JOURNALS FOR PUPILS

i) *Mathematical Pie* is published termly and is aimed at lower secondary pupils. It contains many interesting and useful articles, games and puzzles.

ii) *Plus* is also published termly and is for upper school pupils. Both can be purchased in bulk from the Association for resale to your pupils.

NEWSLETTER

News and information about the Association's activities, branches and matters of interest nationally and internationally is sent to members in the MA newsletter, published three times a year.

GENERAL

Members may attend the annual conference and any of the seminars organised by the Association, may borrow books from the library housed at Leicester University and may send their problems to be solved by the Problem Bureau.

Members may join their local branch and meet other members in their locality.

The MA awards diplomas for teachers who have followed accredited courses at centres around the country. They are the Diploma in Mathematical Education, the Diploma in the Education of Low Attainers and the Diploma in the Management of Departments of Mathematics in Secondary Schools.

The MA supervises the selection of the British team for International Mathematical Olympiads.

Members are encouraged to become actively involved in the MA by writing for the journals, becoming members of the various committees (national and local) and by offering their services to Diploma Boards etc..

Since 1871 the Mathematical Association has provided a forum for all those interested in mathematics and in improving the teaching of mathematics. It is run, voluntarily, by teachers, lecturers and other mathematicians. There is a small permanent staff at the Headquarters in Leicester, from where the Association continues to expand its work of improving the teaching of mathematics.

Reports of interest include:

Why, What and How? (Goals for teaching mathematics, 1976) 50p
Notation and Language in School Mathematics (1977) 50p
Evaluation: of what, by whom, for what purpose? (1979) £1.00
Interface (Primary/secondary and others 1983) £1.50
Teaching Mathematics (Career information, 1984) 75p
Maths Talk (1987) £3.95
Sharing Mathematics with Parents (1986) £2.95
Starting as a Mathematics Teacher (Revised 1986) £1.00
Will Mathematics Count? (1987) £2.00
400+ Questions: A Mathematics In-service Handbook (1988)

BOOK LISTS

Full list (95p) also Teaching Method and Mathematical Education (60p), Pupils with Special Needs (50p), Books for use with Gifted Children (60p)

The Association has also produced:

Video (Working Mathematically with Low Attainers)
Disc and handbook (132 Short Programs)
Posters and postcards
Stickers, badges and sweaters

Further details of services and membership are available from The Mathematical Association, 259 London Road, Leicester LE2 3BE (0533 703877).

Glossary

ASE	Association for Science Education
ATM	Association of Teachers of Mathematics
AUMET	Association of University Mathematics Education Teachers
BTEC	Business and Technician Education Council
CATE	Council for the Accreditation of Teacher Education
CNAA	Council for National Academic Awards
CSE	Certificate of Secondary Education
DES	Department of Education and Science
FE	Further Education
GAIM	Graduated Assessment in Mathematics
GCE	General Certificate of Education
GCSE	General Certificate of Secondary Education
GRIST	Grant Related In-Service Training
HMI	Her Majesty's Inspector
HoD	Head of Department
ILEA	Inner London Education Authority
IMA	Institute of Mathematics and its Applications
INSET	Inservice Education and Training
LEA	Local Education Authority
MA	Mathematical Association
MEI	Mathematics in Education and Industry
NAMA	National Association of Mathematics Advisers
NATFHE	National Association of Teachers in Further and Higher Education
OCEA	Oxford Certificate of Educational Achievement
OU	Open University
PGCE	Post Graduate Certificate in Education
SCAMES	Standing Committee of Associations concerned with Mathematics Education in Schools
SMILE	Secondary Mathematics Individualised Learning Experiment
SMP	School Mathematics Project
TES	Times Educational Supplement

NOTES

NOTES